£5-50

THE CARLTON CLUB

S<small>IR</small> CHARLES PETRIE, B<small>T</small>.

THE

CARLTON

CLUB

With a Preface by
T<small>HE</small> L<small>ORD</small> T<small>WEEDSMUIR</small>
C.B.E.

WHITE LION PUBLISHERS
LONDON AND NEW YORK
1972

Sir Charles Petrie, Bt.
THE CARLTON CLUB
© Copyright, Sir Charles Petrie, 1955, 1972
First published in the United Kingdom by
Eyre and Spottiswoode, 1955

This new and revised White Lion edition
first published 1972

SBN 85617 881 0

Published by White Lion Publishers Limited
138 Park Lane, London W1
and printed in Great Britain by
Biddles of Guildford

Contents

Plates

Preface

THIS NEW EDITION of the history of the Carlton Club will be welcomed by all members. It is 17 years since Sir Charles Petrie first published this work, and these years have seen many changes. Few can now remember the Club of Edwardian days, or the election of Bonar Law as the Conservative Party Leader in 1911, which took place under the roof of the Carlton Club, as did the Party's decision to leave Lloyd George's Coalition in 1922.

The Club has always mirrored the changes in the Party. No longer does it possess the political power which once made it the equivalent of what the Smoking-Room of the House of Commons is today; but many of those who guide the destinies of the present-day Party use the Club regularly, and it is by far the most important political club in the world. Its membership has broadened, as the Party Membership has broadened, and we are a truly National Party, which Disraeli regarded as essential if we were to command power, or indeed, survive.

Since the issue of the first edition the cost of running the Club has continued to rise steadily, as the value of money has fallen, so that the pre-1914 war subscription of 15 guineas is equivalent in current value to over £70. We have suffered, as have all other London Clubs, from a change of habits; men tend to use their Clubs less often, and today there are few who belong to more than one. Against this trend a Club depends for its survival on the loyalty of its members, the use they make of the premises, and the number and calibre of the new members elected.

TWEEDSMUIR
CARLTON CLUB
May 1972

Introduction

THE history of the Carlton Club is so intimately connected with that of the Tory Party that it has seemed well to give some account of the fortunes of that party before proceeding to relate those of the Club. The great names in the Tory hierarchy down the centuries have always been found, and are still to be found, in the list of members of the Carlton, and it is thus surely appropriate to preface the story of the Club with a description of the background against which it is set.

The first difficulty, however, which faces the historian of the Tory Party is to decide where to begin. He can go back to the seventeenth century and seek its origins in the Civil War, or in the struggle over the Exclusion Bill in the reign of Charles II; if he feels this is too remote he can trace its rise from the decline of Jacobitism, and the consequent acceptance by the Tories of the Revolution Settlement and the House of Hanover; lastly, he can commence his study with Disraeli, who gave the party its modern form, and during whose life much of its existing machinery was devised, as will be shown on a later page. The choice is certainly not an easy one, but the arguments for the earlier, rather than for the later, dates are strong. The Tory, whatever he may have happened to call himself at the time – whether Abhorrer, Conservative, or Unionist – has always been a profound believer in the statement of Sir Walter Raleigh that "the councils to which Time is not called, Time will not ratify". Tradition has always meant much to him, so when he thinks about the matter he tends to feel that he is the co-religionist of those who upheld the cause of Church and King three centuries ago; perhaps, then, it is not too far-fetched to say that the Tory Party was born when Charles I raised his standard at Nottingham on August 22nd, 1642. Of one thing at any rate there can be little doubt, and it is that the inspiration of Charles I on the religious side has since the Second World War been stronger among the younger and more thoughtful Tories than for many a long year.

The circumstances in which the Tory Party came into being are not without interest. The real weakness of Charles I lay in the fact that he was his own worst enemy, and he was quite incapable of working up crowd emotion in his own favour. He could only state the issues as he saw them, not as they might appeal to the average man, which is the secret of successful propaganda. He realized neither his own weakness nor his opponents' strength, and he thought that the monarchy was what it had been in the days of the Tudors; while, like many another king both before and since, he mistook the lip-service that was paid to him for true loyalty. Charles also committed the blunder, unpardonable in a statesman, of believing what his enemies said. When Pym, Eliot, Hampden, and a score of others talked of the old rights of Parliament, the King thought that they were sincere, and it did not occur to him, being himself a Scot, that when Englishmen wish to bring about some really revolutionary change they are inclined to claim that they are merely reverting to the customs of the past. Charles himself had no thought of departing from the old Constitution, and he took it for granted that the Parliamentary leaders were actuated by the same motive, when in fact they were merely using their devotion to the Constitution as a cloak to disguise their intention of overturning it. As Disraeli very rightly said, the cause for which Hampden died in the field, and Sidney perished upon the scaffold, was the Whig government of England.[1] The immediate consequence of the King's blunders were that when the Long Parliament met he had hardly a friend in either House.

Fortunately for Charles, his very weakness at Westminster proved to be his strength in the country, for his opponents felt themselves so strong that they were tempted to go too far. They must, too, have believed that they were more secure than ever after the revealed incompetence of the Crown in trying to arrest the Five Members in the House of Commons instead of rounding them up in their beds one dark night without a fuss as any efficient twentieth-century government, whether dictatorial or democratic, would have done. For reasons which were by no means wholly admirable, but which do not concern us here, no politician regretted the disappearance of the Courts of High Commission and Star Chamber, and very few murmured when the bishops were deprived of their seats in the House of Lords, but it was a very different matter when the majority in Parliament proceeded to wrest the control of militia from the Crown, and, in return for Scottish help, set about presbyterianizing the Church of England. This provided Charles with a sufficient number of adherents to fight a civil war; and although he lost both the war and his life, the monarchy was saved, and the Tory Party came into existence.

The establishment of the Commonwealth represented the triumph of a faction and the eclipse of the national idea. When the impeachment of the King was being read in Westminster Hall, and the phrase "all the good people of England" was reached, Lady Fairfax cried out from the gallery, "No, nor the hundredth part of them,"[2] and her interruption

[1] cf. *Sybil*, bk. I, ch. 3.
[2] cf. Clarendon: *History of the Rebellion and Civil Wars in England*, bk. XI.

accurately described the state of the country as a whole. "Nine out of every ten men are against you," Oliver Cromwell was once told. "But what," came the unanswerable reply, "if I put a sword into the hand of the tenth man?" Such was the concept of government represented by the new regime, and the opposition to it brought together those who would have none of such a state of affairs. Disraeli claimed that Charles I died for religion and the poor, and although this is to some extent an exaggeration, there is every justification for saying that his opponents were no true friends either to the one or to the other.

Toryism was thus born in a revolutionary age, for as M. Jacques Bainville so truly wrote of the seventeenth century, *"ce 'grand siècle' n'est devenu celui de l'ordre qu'après avoir passé par le désordre"*.[1] In Germany the Thirty Years' War had created a desert; in France, Spain, and Italy there were disturbances which came within an ace of overturning the existing order, while in Britain the disruptive forces gained a greater victory than elsewhere. The earlier Tories never forgot this, and when in due course the existing order in Church and State was threatened by the storm of the French Revolution they showed no hesitation in rallying to its support. They learnt their lesson in the hard school of civil war and military dictatorship, and it was to be long before they forgot it.

The experiment of the Protectorate is an object-lesson for those who would understand English politics, for it represented everything that is, and should be, anathema to the true Tory, namely the rule of a faction that kept one man in power by brute force. Oliver Cromwell realized this fact most clearly, and he did all that he could to get out of so difficult a position. He toyed with the idea of re-establishing

---

[1] *Histoire de France*, p. 209.

the monarchy in his own person, and he attempted to draw up a Constitution that should broaden the basis of his rule, just as Napoleon III was to do two hundred years later. It was all in vain, and during his short reign as Lord Protector there was a gulf between him and the mass of the English people which no Constitutional compromise could bridge. How wide was this gulf can be gauged by the fact that the Cavaliers – the Tories of the next generation – could fight for Philip IV of Spain against him without the great majority of their fellow-countrymen thinking any the worse of them for it. The victories of his incomparable soldiers were the triumphs, not of England, but of the dominant faction. Cromwell was never really a national figure, yet there is this to be said for him: he was under no illusion as to the weakness of his hold upon the supreme power, and he never desired to rule merely in the name of a section. The first of these facts is a tribute to his head, and the second to his heart.

The restoration of Charles II re-established the old conception of the monarchy as the one pre-eminently national institution, and the Tory Party loyally supported that King in his efforts to make the interests of the nation as a whole prevail over those of the factions as represented by the early Whigs. With this steady support Charles was able to achieve his objective. When he was recalled to the throne he had an empty treasury, no army, and a country that for twenty years had been a prey to every sort of disorder, material and intellectual. By 1685 it had recovered from the Civil Wars, and the power of the factions, which more than once since the Restoration had threatened to revive the old disturbances, had been broken, and their leaders were either in their graves or in exile. For the first time for nearly two generations the country was truly at peace.

It was, of course, during the reign of Charles II that the
Tories first acquired their name. When the Exclusion Bill,
directed against James, Duke of York, as a Catholic, was
introduced by the Whigs, the opposition party, from their
protestations of abhorrence, became known as Abhorrers.
Soon, however, they were lampooned by their opponents as
Tories, and the name stuck. It had originally been applied to
Irish Catholic *guerrilleros* earlier in the century, who were
subsequently termed rapparees, and of them a contemporary
wrote, "Lest the next age may not be of the same humour
with this, and the name of a rapparee may possibly be thought
a finer thing than it really is, I do assure you that in my style,
they can never be reputed other than tories, robbers, thieves,
and bogtrotters." The Tories, it may be mentioned, at once
retaliated by referring to the Petitioners for the Exclusion
Bill as Whigs, which is derived from the whiggamores who
were Scottish rebels of the period.

With the accession of James II a new, and unhappy, era
began, for the Tories, the traditional party of Church and
King, found themselves called to choose between the Angli-
can Church and the Roman Catholic King. The intentions
of James were no doubt excellent, both in politics and in
religion, but like all politicians in a hurry he settled nothing
and unsettled everything. The extent of the apprehensions he
created enabled the Whigs, whom his brother had left a
broken and discredited faction, to revive as an effective force,
and even to secure the co-operation of many of their Tory
opponents against a ruler who had united in opposition to his
programme, those influenced by the highest as well as those
activated by the lowest motives that sway mankind. The result
was the Revolution of 1688, which was thus brought about
by a temporary alliance of forces normally in conflict.

As is invariably the case when parties of the Right lend themselves to revolutionary proceedings, the Tories soon found that rebellion to constituted authority is not a tap which can be turned on and off at will. Most of them had probably no other intention than to frighten James back to his brother's ways, but when it was too late they discovered that they had overturned a dynasty, and seated a foreigner on the throne. They were bewildered by the course of events which they had so largely precipitated. Their creed had for more than a generation been summed up in the words "Church and King", and when the King had become an alien they clung all the more steadfastly to the Church. Some frankly regretted what had happened, and sought to undo it, while even those who disclaimed the name of Jacobite had many misgivings. "The loyal were loyal indeed, but in their hearts were many regrets and some unextinguished hopes. In dozens of homes, empty places and smuggled letters would every day remind them of a miserable son loitering on the Boulevards, of a daughter cloistered at Douai, of friends whose hungry idealism reproached their own comfortable apostasy, or of refugees barely kept alive by Papal alms."[1] The Jacobite affiliations of the Tory Party were more or less pronounced as circumstances might dictate, but they continued to exist until the accession of George III.

Such was the state of the Tory Party for more than twenty years after the Revolution, and then, in the autumn of 1710, it suddenly found itself in office again. The country was weary of the War of the Spanish Succession which the Whigs evinced no disposition to bring to an end, while the prosecution of Sacheverell had given their opponents the extremely effective rallying-cry of "The Church in danger". In later

[1] Feiling, K.: *A History of the Tory Party*, 1640–1714, p. 300.

years Bolingbroke was quite frank about the attitude of himself and his friends on this occasion. "I am afraid", he wrote,
"that we came to Court in the same disposition as all parties
have done; that the principal spring of our actions was to
have the government of the State in our hands; that our
principal views were the conservation of this power, great
employment to ourselves, and great opportunities of reward-
ing those who had helped to raise us, and of hurting those
who stood in opposition to us. It is, however, true that with
these considerations of private and party interest there were
others intermingled which had for their object the public
good of the nation – at least, what we took to be such."[1]

The first task before the new Tory government was to
bring the war to a conclusion, and this was in due course
effected by the Treaty of Utrecht in 1713. Although some
of the methods employed to bring this about are open to
serious criticism the responsibility does not, as is sometimes
suggested, rest with Bolingbroke alone, but must be shared
with his Whig predecessors in office who had, for party
reasons, rendered it impossible to conduct negotiations in any
other manner. As for the treaty itself its great merit was its
realism, and thus it was thoroughly in accordance with Tory
principles. France was the first Power on the mainland of
Europe; Philip V was the monarch desired by Spain; Great
Britain was building a colonial empire; and Prussia and Savoy
were rising states: all these incontrovertible realities were admitted at Utrecht. At the same time precautions were taken
against the pre-eminence of France developing into hege-
mony, just as the recognition of Philip was a check to any
Habsburg inclinations in the same direction. It was all
eminently reasonable, and in its main outlines this essentially

[1] *A Letter to Sir William Wyndham.*

Tory settlement endured for more than two generations, which is surely as far ahead as any statesman can be expected to look.

Bolingbroke and his colleagues did not set out to create a new heaven and earth. They ignored general principles; they dealt with the real, not with the ideal; and their work stood. It is true that they abandoned the Catalans, but this betrayal was a small affair compared with, say, that of the Poles at the end of the Second World War. There is, indeed, a great deal to be said against Bolingbroke both in his public and private capacity, but it can hardly be denied that he was a good European, and it was as such that he negotiated the Treaty of Utrecht.

Yet, in spite of this achievement in the field of foreign policy, the Tory Party was on the eve of a catastrophe even greater than those which it was to experience in 1832, 1906, and 1945, and this in spite of the fact that at a General Election in the summer of 1713 the government's majority was practically unimpaired. The reason for this disaster was that, with Anne in failing health, the party was once more called upon to choose between Church and King, and it could not make up its mind. The solution first favoured was that the exiled James III should become a Protestant, and reign as a Tory monarch in much the same way as George I was to do as a Whig one. This plan broke down because James, unlike his ancestor Henry IV of France, refused to change his religion for the sake of a throne. On the other hand, he was perfectly willing to give any reasonable assurances in the matter of the religion of others if he was allowed to practise his own. "All the just securities that can reasonably be asked for your religion, liberties, and properties I shall be most willing to grant, and as that can be expected from a man of principle and true honour I am ready to comply with it, and you know I have too much of both to require more of me."[1]

The refusal of James to change his religion placed the government in a serious dilemma, for there was no hope of effecting a legal restoration while he was a Roman Catholic. A *coup d'état* might have been possible, but it was doubtful whether there would be time for the necessary preparation in view of the state of the Queen's health, quite apart from the probability that some of the more timid ministers, such as Oxford, might shrink from the use of force. There can also be little doubt but that the refusal of James to leave his Church weakened the desire of Bolingbroke and the less disinterested members of the Tory Party to have him on the throne. As Bolingbroke was later to write, "The Tories looked at a restoration of the Stuarts as a sure means to throw the whole power of government into their hands. I am confident that they would have found themselves deceived."[2] In this Bolingbroke was right, for with all his failings James was both too honest a man, and had too shrewd an appreciation of the true principles of monarchy, ever to reign as the head of a faction, which was in reality all that Bolingbroke and some of his friends required of him.

As there was no hope of obtaining James on Tory terms, and as the Elector of Hanover was in the hands of the Whigs, the only course open to Bolingbroke was to get complete control of the machinery of government, and then to bargain with the two claimants. He therefore embarked upon this policy, but time was not vouchsafed to him to carry it through to a successful conclusion. On Sunday, August 1st,

[1] cf. Trevelyan, G. M.: *England Under Queen Anne*, vol. III, pp. 266–69.
[2] *A Letter to Sir William Wyndham.*

1714, Anne died, and Bolingbroke wrote to Swift, "The Earl of Oxford was removed on Tuesday, the Queen died on Sunday. What a world this is, and how does fortune banter us." Many legends are current as to what happened that Sunday morning in Kensington, but whatever may have been plotted George I was duly proclaimed King without the slightest opposition.

The accession of the House of Hanover marked the end of what may be described as the first Tory Party. As we have seen, the Revolution of 1688 had dealt it a severe blow, but it had recovered during the last years of Anne. It was never to be the same again after this second catastrophe. The Tories proceeded to split into factions which ranged from those who accepted the new dynasty to Jacobites who saw no hope save in the successful application of physical force. No leader appeared who could unite these discordant groups, and the consequence was that for two generations the Whigs ruled the country. All this time, however, it is to be noted that the Tory strength, particularly in the rural areas, was unimpaired, and in 1743 the Whig Pulteney estimated that two-thirds of the nation was Tory. When, therefore, during the latter part of the eighteenth century, the Whigs in their turn began to split into factions, Toryism soon showed signs of a revival. In the meantime its leaders remained in their country houses, and lived the sort of life which Fielding depicted in his portrait of Squire Western.

So there came into existence that "Venetian Constitution" which Disraeli was to deride in the following century. Oligarchs habitually destroy the souls of the nations they govern, and England under the rule of the Whigs was certainly no exception. The spiritual idea was eliminated from the civil government, and the triumph of Erastianism resulted in the secularization of the Church together with a utilitarian theory of political life, so that when a religious revival did take place it was driven out of the bounds of the Establishment. No doubt a reaction against the turmoil of the previous hundred years was due, but this would not have taken the form it did had not every sort of enthusiasm been sternly repressed by those in office. It may be all very well to let sleeping dogs lie, but it is another matter to drug every dog deliberately with a view to keeping it in a permanent state of somnolence, which was the policy of Walpole. In Ireland and Scotland the results of the Whig rule were still more deadly, and in the case of Ireland the legacy that it bequeathed to the future could not have been more disastrous. Those who wish to estimate the exact benefits which were at this time conferred on the inhabitants of the British Isles would do well to forsake the glowing accounts to be found in the pages of Oldmixon, Macaulay, and Trevelyan, for the study of the Newgate Calendar, the pictures of Hogarth, and the working of the Penal Laws in Ireland. On the other hand, those who supported the ruling oligarchy had nothing of which to complain, and it is only now, after two World Wars, that their descendants are being compelled to dispose of the vast palaces and the broad acres that were the reward for keeping Whiggery in power.

Next to the Church, the monarchy was the chief sufferer. The Whig policy was to put the Crown back where it had been at the time of the Wars of the Roses, that is to say to reduce it to the mere leadership of a faction, but at first this project was not wholly successful. William III and Anne were determined not to be the puppets of any one party, and as there was always the possibility that either of these monarchs might come to some arrangement with the legitimate heir for his eventual succession, the Whigs had to refrain from pushing them too far. When, however, the House of Hanover came to the throne in the person of George I the case was very different, and the dominant oligarchy did not hesitate to apply the screw; while the Fifteen strengthened its hand by demonstrating how unpopular the new dynasty really was. For many years after 1715 it was quite clear that a change of the party in power would mean a change in the person of the monarch.

It is not surprising that in due course there should grow up a reaction against this state of affairs, and it was initiated in 1749 by Bolingbroke when he published *The Idea of a Patriot King* for the edification of Frederick, Prince of Wales. The book is an appeal to discard the party system and everything for which it stands. According to the author "a limited monarchy is the best of governments", and a hereditary monarchy the best of monarchies. "The good of the people is the ultimate and true end of government", and "the greatest good of a people is their liberty." The best way to provide for the continuance of that liberty is by securing the accession of a Patriot King, who will not rule by divine right, but who will also not be the mere figurehead of an oligarchical faction. He will be a constitutional monarch, whose power is limited by his consent to exercise that power subject to public opinion expressed in a free Parliament. Under him corruption will cease, for a Patriot King had no reason to be corrupt. "He is the most powerful of all reformers, for he is himself a sort of standing miracle so rarely seen, and so little understood, that the sure effects of his appearance will be admiration and love in every honest breast, confusion and terror to every guilty conscience, but submission and resignation in all."

A great part of this famous treatise had no other purpose than to flatter the Prince of Wales, who might one day be in a position to take Bolingbroke as his Prime Minister, and to belabour the Whigs. Yet much of it is of permanent value, and has had its effect upon English history. The conception of the monarch standing above the parties, and representing the national interest as opposed to purely factional interests, has been the Tory interpretation of the kingly office ever since. It is true that those who have called themselves Tories, or Conservatives, have not always been true to this principle, but that does not affect the issue. Disraeli, in particular, based his policy of *Imperium et Libertas* upon *The Idea of a Patriot King*.

It was not, however, Frederick, but his son George III, who attempted to put into practice the theories of Boling-broke, and in spite of the disability under which he suffered of not being the legitimate sovereign he succeeded to no in-considerable extent. The decline of Jacobitism assisted him in a marked degree, since it regained for the ruling monarch the support of those who were naturally the bulwark of his throne, but who had been in opposition to it for two genera-tions. Furthermore, the Whig oligarchy was becoming divi-ded and enfeebled, and after the collapse of the Elibank Plot in 1753 had shown that the danger from the Jacobites was at an end, the Whigs could no longer claim that they alone stood between England and a Popish Pretender. George III, too, if a man devoid of the higher gifts of statesmanship, knew exactly what he wanted, and this gave him a decided advantage over many of his opponents. He undoubtedly intended to be a Patriot King of the Bolingbroke type, and by the exercise of the royal authority to ensure that the quarrels of the factions were subordinated to the interests of the nation. For over twenty years he devoted all his energies to this end, and though he was far from achieving his object-tive, his motives were never ignoble.

In this task he was greatly assisted by the revival of the Tory Party. It was in many ways a different Toryism from that of Stuart times; there was more insistence on loyalty to the Constitution and to the throne as an institution than to the monarch personally, and very little was now heard about the Church. The fact was that if the Tories had sacrificed many of their old principles, they still retained their devotion to the throne, and, despairing of the restoration of the Stuarts, they were now prepared to transfer their loyalty to the House of Hanover. As Burke put it, "They changed their idol but they preserved their idolatry." George III did everything he could to make this easy, and there was soon a strong body of opinion throughout the country which was prepared to support him in any attempt to increase the power of the Crown. In addition, there was the fact that even without straining the Constitution he was in a very strong position, so that it is not surprising that before long he was able to shake off the domination of the Whigs. They were not, of course, what they had been earlier in the century, or the King would not have been able even to embark upon his project, and all the forces of the State would have been employed to repress any Tory revival.

In the main the Tories supported George III loyally throughout the first twenty years of his reign, and when the Younger Pitt, although himself of Whig origin, became Prime Minister at the end of 1783 they rallied to him. Six years later their cohesion and their appeal to their fellow-countrymen were both immensely enhanced by the outbreak of the French Revolution, and as the details of the atrocities perpetrated across the Channel became known in England there was a revulsion of feeling against the Whigs which was to keep them out of office for forty years, save for one brief interval. Much of this was due to Edmund Burke, who, with Bolingbroke, has been one of the leading intellectual forces in the moulding of the Tory creed. Let it be said at once that Burke's earlier views, especially at the time of the War of American Independence, are capable of a very different interpretation, but however this may be he was one of the earliest to appreciate the significance of what was happening in France. It is not altogether easy to account for his influence over the British public, but for the last years of his life it was very considerable indeed. During the brief period in which he held office he had not been a success, and he generally emptied the House of Commons when he rose to speak. His manner and appearance, too, were against him, for he had a very strong brogue; and Wilkes said of him that just as the Venus of Apelles suggested milk and honey, so Burke's oratory was reminiscent of whiskey and potatoes, while the dandies of Brooks's and White's laughed at his large spectacles, ill-fitting brown coat, and bob-wig.

Nevertheless when Burke got a pen in his hand it was a different matter, as was shown in 1790, the year in which he published his *Reflections on the French Revolution*. It was one of those books that come just at the moment when the ordinary reader is beginning to think along the lines they indicate, and its success was instantaneous. Although it was published at five shillings no fewer than seven thousand copies were sold in six days. The King was delighted, and told everyone, "Read it; it will do you good; it is a book which every gentleman ought to read." The force of Burke's arguments was not lost upon the Whigs, for they began to split, and before long the larger proportion of them were to be found supporting Pitt. That this should have been the case was largely due to Burke, for he had followed up his earlier work on the French Revolution with *An Appeal from New to Old Whigs* and *Letters on a Regicide Peace*. As his prophecies came true his influence naturally increased, and the Duke of Portland, Windham, and others crossed the floor. Not long afterwards Burke died with the satisfaction of having succeeded in his object. When Canning heard of his death he wrote, "There is only one piece of news, but that is news for the world – Burke is dead."

The opening years of the nineteenth century were marked by several governments whose tenure of office proved to be short lived for a variety of reasons which do not concern us here, and the last of them was the Whig administration of "All the Talents", which fell in 1807. From that date until 1830 the Tory Party was continually in office, so that it can justly claim credit for all the remarkable achievements of those years. First and foremost among them was the defeat of Napoleon, and then the resettlement of Europe after his downfall. In face of the furious opposition of the Whigs, and the lukewarm attitude of many of its own followers, the Tory government loyally supported Wellington until the great day came when he crossed the Pyrenees, and a victorious British army stood on French soil. Then followed the Congress of Vienna, and another Tory peace. "The settlement of 1815 was enduring; it did what it intended to do, and preserved the balance of power in Europe for a hundred years. It was based on realities, not on desires; on what was possible, not on what we liked to think possible. The problem was not to create a world of free, self-determined nationalities but an enduring balance of Great Powers. In so doing the Treaty of

INTRODUCTION

Vienna added more to the sum of future happiness than any other diplomatic instrument in history. . . . It was the supreme merit of the architects of the settlement of 1815, who were also responsible for the peaceful evolution of the twelve years which followed, that they saw the nature of the new problem, and found a solution."[1]

We are now come to the period immediately preceding the foundation of the Carlton Club, so it will behove us to regard the political scene somewhat more closely, for it was the one in which its originators had their being: only seventeen years elapsed between Waterloo and the inauguration of the Carlton.

The Britain which emerged from the long struggle with France was a very different country from that which had entered the war twenty-two years before. She was far more industrialized, and this change had produced problems of an economic and social nature which called for solution: furthermore, the external danger to which the nation had for so long been exposed had had the effect of postponing reform. Thus there was at one and the same time an ugly feeling of unrest, especially in the industrial areas, and a tendency in other quarters to regard any concession as dangerous. Even while hostilities were in progress there had been widespread discontent, and with the coming of peace it was intensified. In effect, the government of the day, of which the Earl of Liverpool had been the head since the murder of Perceval in 1812, was confronted with a very delicate situation indeed, and its task was not rendered any easier by the absence of all precedents to guide it, a fact which its critics have tended to ignore.

In these circumstances it was hardly surprising that with the arrival of peace many chickens, some of whom had grown

[1] Jerrold, D.: *England; Past, Present, and Future*, pp. 117–18.

into large and singularly ill-omened birds, should have come home to roost. Then, too, the years which immediately followed the war were marked by acute distress and by a general feeling of insecurity. The golden age to which many had looked forward seemed as remote as ever, and the resulting disillusionment was bitter. As always on such occasions, the desire for reform was confused with incitement to revolution, and alarm spread rapidly among all who had anything to lose. Political power still rested in the hands of the great landowners and of those country gentlemen who appear on the pages of Jane Austen: such men not unnaturally wanted a period of calm after the disturbances of the previous twenty years, and they had no sympathy with the agitators who wished to take advantage of the coming of peace to effect sweeping changes in the Constitution. Nor was this all, for any advocate of reform was liable to come under suspicion: it was not forgotten that the French Revolution had had relatively modest beginnings, and the attitude of those in authority not unnaturally was that if the reformers were given an inch they would take an ell. Therefore they were inclined to harden their hearts against all concessions, thereby very nearly precipitating the crisis which they were most anxious to avoid. Five years after Waterloo that shrewd old man Louis XVIII was writing to his ambassador in London that the progress of events in Britain formed a close parallel with what had happened in France thirty-one years before.[1]

For everything that went wrong during this period the Tory Prime Minister, Lord Liverpool, was posthumously to incur the formidable displeasure of Disraeli, who did his best to hand him down to posterity deprived of every shred of reputation for statesmanship. The unfortunate Premier was

[1] cf. Daudet, E.: *L'Ambassade du Duc Decazes en Angleterre*, p. 129.

satirized as the "Arch-Mediocrity", and sneering references were made to his "meagre diligence". The government "fell into a panic", Disraeli declared, "having fulfilled during their lives the duties of administration, they were frightened because they were called upon, for the first time, to perform the functions of government. Like all weak men, they had recourse to what they called strong measures. They determined to put down the multitude. They thought they were imitating Mr. Pitt, because they mistook disorganization for sedition."[1] Disraeli himself, it may be remarked, never had to deal with problems of anything like the magnitude of those which confronted the man whom he thus abused; but for the present generation the case is very different, and there is naturally both more understanding and more sympathy for the man who had first to conduct a major war, and then to deal with its aftermath, than was to be found among the Victorians who lived in an age of prosperity and security.

Yet, when the matter is regarded objectively, it must surely be admitted that no man who was merely the incompetent functionary depicted by Disraeli could have controlled a team containing such personalities as Canning, Castlereagh, Eldon, Huskisson, Peel, Palmerston, and, above all, Wellington himself. The Tory government over which Liverpool presided for so many years was one of the most brilliant Britain has ever known, and beside the names of its members those of Disraeli's ministers appear dwarfs indeed. Such being the case it is difficult to disagree with Mr. Keith Feiling's judgment that "this over-worked Prime Minister has been pilloried long enough for the faults of millowners and justices; for severities in which he was overborne by Eldon, for omis-

[1] *Coningsby*, bk. II, ch. I.

sions which he shared with Peel".[1] A more recent authority, Mr. Brock, has gone even further: "Men will not suffer for long the leadership of a man who is no more than an amiable party manager, and the backing of authority must be sound principles and solid ideas. . . . Sound judgment was one of his principal qualifications for high office, and it was this which could take him out of the politician and make him a statesman."[2]

What the critics of the Victorian era, who had not been called upon to deal with the aftermath of a great war, were inclined to forget was that the Tory ministry had been one of the prime factors in the overthrow of Napoleon, and its members would have been more than human if they had not thought that this entitled them to control their country's destinies during the years of peace which followed the victory. Furthermore, the vast majority of the electors took the same line, for whatever posterity may think of Sidmouth and his Six Acts, he and his colleagues continued to be returned to power at successive elections. Whatever, too, may be said for or against the repressive measures of that time on grounds of ethics or expediency, they were what the voters wanted. Nor, it should be remarked, was the government "called upon to deal merely with merry peasants and innocuous idealists,"[3] for there were desperate schemes afoot in some quarters. The men who organized the Cato Street Conspiracy, and the rising that ended at Bonnymuir, were dangerous revolutionaries against whom the use of force was inevitable.

It may well be that the government made a mistake in not discriminating more carefully between the different classes of

[1] *Sketches in Nineteenth Century Biography*, p. 31.
[2] *Lord Liverpool and Liberal Toryism*, p. 33.
[3] Feiling, K.: *Sketches in Nineteenth Century Biography*, p. 27.

reformers, but their fault was the same as that of every administration in similar circumstances: Pitt had been no wiser, and the history of our own age abounds in instances of panic-stricken measures being adopted towards those suspected of harbouring designs inimical to the safety of the State, however innocent their motives may have been in reality. Liverpool had witnessed the storming of the Bastille with his own eyes, and he and his colleagues had at any rate the excuse that they had seen in France the result of looking on helplessly while the agitation grew. Furthermore, the government might have felt justified in adopting more moderate measures had they received any support from the Opposition in the maintenance of law and order; but although in private the Whigs might deplore the more violent excesses of the Radicals, in public they did nothing to discourage, and much to stimulate, them. It has also to be recalled that there was still no effective police force, and that a minor disturbance could easily assume dangerous proportions before it was checked.

So for twelve years after Waterloo the Tory ministry grappled not only with the consequences of war and of the Industrial Revolution, but also with the liability caused by the presence at the Head of the State of the so-called "First Gentleman of Europe" first as Regent and then as George IV. By the end of that time the country was set upon the road to that unexampled prosperity which was to last until the end of the century, and almost to the eve of the First World War. Then disaster came once more upon the long dominant Tory Party. For nearly forty-four years the Tories had been almost continuously in power, and then in the spring of 1827 Liverpool had a stroke which completely incapacitated him, and from the effects of which he died in the following year.

It was soon seen that no one except the much-maligned Prime Minister could hold his party together. "The Hundred Days" of Canning ensued, but even that great statesman had to have recourse to the Whigs before he could form a ministry, for several leading Tories, such as Wellington, refused to serve under him. Canning in his turn died, and then came Goderich, "the transient and embarrassed phantom" of Disraeli's gibe, and finally Wellington himself.

None of them proved able to fill Liverpool's place, and with the agitation for Reform sweeping the country the Tories, with their own ranks hopelessly divided, went down to disaster. At the General Election of 1832, held on the new franchise, only 179 Tories were returned out of a total membership of the House of Commons of 658. In these circumstances it was little wonder that they should have sought to establish a rallying place, for they had clearly reached a crisis in their history, and their situation was comparable with what it had been in 1714, and was again to be in 1906 and 1945. Such was the political background against which the foundation of the Carlton Club was set.

CHAPTER I

Early Years

THE foundation of the Carlton Club took place on March 10th, 1832, when a general meeting of the Tory Club was held at the Thatched House Tavern, with the Marquess of Salisbury[1] in the chair. At this meeting a committee[2] was appointed for two main purposes: the first was "to look out for and take a House for the Club forthwith"; and the second was "to submit to the next General Meeting Rules and Regulations for the Management of the Club". At this further meeting, held on March 17th, a set of rules and regulations was adopted, and in the first of these the Club was officially designated the Carlton Club.

Such are the facts, but it was not long before legends grew up which were completely at variance with them, and some of these legends long found credence. They probably had their origin in some paragraphs which appeared in the *Illustrated Times* on March 15th, 1856:

You want to know the history of the Carlton Club. Indeed! So deep a mystery and secrecy has enshrouded its operations that there are very few people in this establishment, not even that elderly gentleman who is scolding the waiter as if he were the

---

[1] The 2nd Marquess. Born 1791, died 1868. He married the daughter and heiress of Bamber Gascoyne of Childwall Hall, Lancashire. He took by Royal Licence the name of Gascoyne, and was empowered to sign that name before all titles of honour, as can be seen from his signature in the minute books.

[2] For its composition, cf. Appendix I.

parent of the club, could tell you a tittle of it. Look into Peter Cunningham's *Handbook of London*. Peter has not a word to say about the origin or history of the Carlton, though he is great upon the granite pillars outside, and the resemblance to Sansovino's library, and so forth. Ask the *Builder*, the correct, well-informed, respectable *Builder*. The *Builder* will tell you that the Carlton Club was founded by the Duke of Wellington in 1831. No such thing. The Carlton Club was founded in 1828, the first year of his Premiership, by the Iron Duke, in association with the late Sir Robert Peel, the Marquess of Salisbury, the Earl of Jersey, the late Messrs. Goulburn and Herries, Billy Holmes (so long the Tory Whipper-in), and Bonham, afterwards of the Ordnance, of painful notoriety.

The club opened house very quietly and unostentatiously in Charles Street, St. James's Square, the street made illustrious by the residence of Edmund Burke, and where the poet Crabbe waited upon the author of the *Reflections* with the letter which has become memorable in literary history. It was the time when Catholic Emancipation was preparing, and the Great Duke wished to have some better organization afloat than the Brunswick and Protestant Clubs, which even Lord Eldon could not stomach. The name of "Carlton" was chosen to designate the attachment of the members of the Club to the politics of his late Most Gracious Majesty George IV, whose residence, Carlton House, had recently been pulled down.

This account of the origin of the Carlton Club is highly imaginative and almost wholly inaccurate, but for long it obtained support in the less responsible quarters. In reality, the foundation of a club dates from the time when its potential members meet together and call it into existence, as happened in the case of the Carlton on March 10th, 1832. That there was an institution called the Tory Club already in existence is obvious, and it may well have originated in the circumstances related in the *Illustrated Times*, but that club was not the Carlton as it has subsequently been known.

In any event the great age of the London club was dawning. The Travellers, originally started in 1814, was one of the earliest of its class, and it was soon followed by others; so that by 1832 the United Service, the Guards', the Oriental, the Athenaeum, and the Garrick, to mention only a few names, were already in existence. The demolition of Carlton House had left a number of suitable sites for building, and as the area of Pall Mall and St. James's had long been the centre of coffee-house life, it was only natural that these new establishments, which were the successors of the coffee-houses, should concentrate there. Nor did they lack members in the new world which was coming into existence. For better or for worse the narrow and exclusive aristocratic society of the eighteenth century, which had revolved round Brooks' and White's, was breaking up, or rather it was being permeated and expanded by that middle class into whose hands political power was passing. Furthermore, although London was rapidly growing, the difficulties of transport prevented residence too far from Westminster or the City, and so there arose a demand for clubs and the amenities which they provided. So long as this state of affairs obtained the West End clubs flourished; when it changed they began to decline.

As we have seen, the first task imposed upon the Committee was to find premises, and this problem they proceeded to solve by taking a short lease of Lord Kensington's house at No. 2 Carlton Terrace. There the Club remained until the end of 1835, and in the following year it moved into a new building which Sir Robert Smirke designed on a piece of land in Pall Mall at the corner of what is now Carlton Gardens. The Committee had hoped that it would prove possible to go direct from Lord Kensington's house to the new premises, but these were not ready in time, and Lord

Kensington refused to extend the lease beyond the end of
1835. Alternative temporary accommodation had, accordingly, to be sought, and so we read in the committee minutes
of December 15th, 1835, that it was decided to make the
following announcement to the members:

> Members are informed that in consequence of the lease of this
> house expiring on the 25th instant and of a negotiation with Lord
> Kensington for any prolonged occupation of it having failed it
> will be necessary to close the Coffee Room after Thursday next
> and the Reading Room after Tuesday the 22nd inst.
> The Architect having reported that in consequence of some
> unavoidable interruptions that have occurred, the new house will
> not be ready for the reception of the Club before the middle of
> the ensuing month the Committee have taken apartments for the
> intervening period at the Carlton Hotel in Regent Street which
> will be open to Members on the morning of the 23rd instant.

Although this was the first time that the members of the
Club had to be temporarily accommodated in a hotel, it was
not the last; for during the Second World War, when the
Club was closed in the summer for the servants' holidays, and
the other West End clubs were too crowded to offer the
hospitality traditional on such occasions, facilities for members were arranged in Brown's Hotel in Dover Street.

Ten years later premises adjoining the Club on the west
side were taken, and extensive alterations and improvements
were made by Mr. Sidney Smirke, a brother of Sir Robert,
while in 1854 it was decided to take the whole building down,
and to replace it with the one that remained until it was
bombed in 1940. Contemporaries were not very flattering to
the taste of the committee, for of the first club-house the
Illustrated London News wrote that it was "of poor Grecian
design"; while of the second, which was with a few varia-

tions the facsimile of the Libreria Vecchia at Venice by Sansovino, a critic in Weale's *London* said that the original was "a work whose celebrity converts into admiration the censure that this imitation of it would, were it an original composition, else incur for the monstrousness of its proportions, and violation of all orthodoxy and rule: nothing less monstrous, in fact, can the Ionic, or upper order, be pronounced, if it be tested by ordinary rules, especially as it is considerably more ponderous than that of the Doric order below". Another critic condemned the adaptation of Sansovino's work as "not creditable to English art, or even politic as to intended effort. Some of the best features are omitted in the copy, and, of course, any defects that there are become doubly reprehensible in the work of a copyist". It may be added that in time the facing stonework of the building became seriously affected by the atmosphere of London, and in 1912 it was decided to reface it with Portland stone. This work was delayed owing to the First World War, and it was not finally completed until 1924.

What is curious about the Club in its early days is that no object of its existence is laid down in the rules. It was clearly founded to fight the supporters of the Reform Bill and to serve as a rallying point for the Tories, yet one of its original members, Thomas Raikes, could write in his diary under date April 7th, 1832: "A new Tory club has just been formed, for which Lord Kensington's house in Carlton Gardens has been taken. Lord Clanwilliam[1] and others having asked me to belong to it; though no party man or political character,

[1] The 3rd Earl. Born 1795, died 1879. Private Secretary to Castlereagh at the Foreign Office, 1817-19. Under-Secretary of State for Foreign Affairs, 1822-23. Lord Ronald Gower, in his *Reminiscences*, says he was "as handsome at 70 as when Lawrence painted him forty years before, and full of the charm of high spirits that not even old age could quench".

I have agreed." Disraeli, on the other hand, regarded the Club as the recognized social citadel of Toryism, and when he definitely joined the Tory Party after his defeat at High Wycombe in 1835 his first step was to get his name put down for the Carlton. He was proposed by Viscount Strangford and seconded by the Marquess of Chandos. He certainly neglected no effort to get himself elected, for in February 1836 he is found canvassing Lady Blessington:

My dearest Lady,
Early in March there are to be fifty members elected into the Carlton by the members at large. A strong party of my friends, Lord L., Lord Chandos, Stuart de Rothesay, etc., are very active in my behalf, and I think among the leaders of our party my claims would be recognized; but doubtless there is a sufficient alloy of dunces even among the Conservatives, and I have no doubt there will be a strong opposition to me. Although I will not canvass myself, I wish my friends to do so *most earnestly*. I know from personal experience that one word from you would have more effect upon me than letters from all the lords in Xdom. I wish therefore to enlist you on my side, and will take the liberty of sending you a list tomorrow.

Votre Dis.

Disraeli was successful, and he lost no time in announcing the good news to his sister Sarah: "I carried the Carlton; the opposition was not considerable in committee, but my friends were firm – 400 candidates, and all in their opinion with equal claims." What is more, he enjoyed the Club when he had been elected, as he told his sister a few weeks later:

The Carlton
April 18
The Opera is very good this year, and Carlotta Grisi the great dancer. There is a report in *Times* of the Lewes banquet. About my pledging myself to come forward is a mendacious flourish, but

does not matter. The Carlton is a great lounge, and I have found a kind friend in Francis Baring[1] – Lord Ashburton's eldest son.

His rival of the future, Gladstone, had been elected three years earlier, on March 6th, 1833, though it is a curious coincidence, if nothing more, that both in the committee minutes and in the letter from the secretary informing him of his election his initials are omitted, and he appears merely as – Gladstone, M.P.

It may be that the absence of any reference in the rules to the political opinions of the members was due to a desire not to embarrass those who belonged to the Royal Family, for the names of the Dukes of Cumberland and Gloucester appear in the List of Members for 1832. They are repeated in that of the following year, but in 1834 the name of the Duke of Gloucester is deleted, though that of the Earl of Munster, the son of the reigning monarch, William IV, makes its appearance. Cumberland kept his name on the books even after he became King of Hanover in 1837, for in those days there was no rule to the effect that a member must be a British subject. As for political views, it was not until 1912 that it was definitely laid down in the rules that all new members must belong to the Conservative and Unionist Party, though it is to be noted that on July 28th, 1857, it was resolved that the following letter be sent to the Proposer and Seconder of all prospective members:

I am directed by the Committee of Management to request that you will acquaint me if the political views of——are strictly

[1] Later the 5th Lord Ashburton. Born 1800, died 1868. He married the daughter of the Duc de Bassano. M.P. for Thetford, 1830–31, 1832–41, and 1848–57. He left £250,000. Of his family the Duc de Richelieu said: "There are six Great Powers in Europe – England, France, Austria, Russia, Prussia, and Baring Brothers."

in accordance with those entertained by the great body of the Carlton Club.

Of one thing there can be no question, and it is that in those early days the committee worked very hard indeed. Nothing was too insignificant for their attention. The addition of a single weekly provincial newspaper to the number of periodicals taken by the Club was considered a matter worthy of their notice, and there are repeated resolutions to the effect that no servant, however menial, must be engaged or dismissed without their approval. During what may be described as the formative period of the Club's life the committee met once a week, even in August and September, for there would not appear to have been any annual closing in those days; and on February 6th, 1838, it was resolved: "That until further notice the committee meets on Saturdays at 3 o'clock instead of Tuesdays" – a resolution which proves that the weekend habit was still very much in the future. There was, it may be remarked, no Chairman of the Club until Lord Claud Hamilton was elected to this position in 1913; before then the chair at meetings of the committee does not seem to have been taken on any very settled plan.

That there was plenty of work for the committee to do in these circumstances goes without saying, and the last item in the minutes of the meeting held on Boxing Day 1832 (the fact that a meeting was held at all on this day is a curious commentary on the habits of the age) is concerned with a relatively trivial matter, viz., "The Steward was spoken to on account of a complaint of the Fish being bad made by the Marquess of Salisbury." In due course it was decided to delegate some of the more detailed work to sub-committees, and in March 1834, three of these were called into existence; it is not without interest to note how they were constituted:

Servants	Books and Newspapers
Marquess of Tweeddale	The Right Hon. Sir Henry Hardinge,
Lord Redesdale	M.P.
Sir Alexander Grant, Bt.	Mr. Lockhart[1]
Lord Saltoun	The Right Hon.T . Frankland Lewis,
Lord Granville Somerset,	M.P.
M.P.	Mr. Bonham, M.P.
	The Right Hon. Charles Herries,
	M.P.
	Viscount Strangford
	Marquess of Salisbury
	Earl De La Warr

Wine

Marquess of Graham
Earl of Wicklow
Sir Alexander Grant, Bt.
Earl of Mansfield
The Right Hon. T. Frankland Lewis, M.P.

The names are in order in which they appear in the relevant minutes.

The appointment of a sub-committee so early in the Club's life to look after the books and periodicals is significant of the interest which was taken by the General Committee in building up a library. There are continual references to the purchase of books and Parliamentary reports and papers, and in May 1837 the annual general meeting passed two resolutions on the subject:

(1) That a sum of not less than £300 annually be expended in the purchase of books, exclusive of periodicals.

(2) That a committee of five members be named by the General Committee for the management of the library, and of the funds devoted to the purchase of books.

[1] The biographer of Sir Walter Scott.

At their next meeting the General Committee implemented
these resolutions by appointing a Library Committee consisting of Lord Francis Egerton, Viscount Mahon, Viscount
Strangford, Mr. S. Jackson, and Mr. W. E. Gladstone, M.P.
In this way were laid the foundations of that library which
was one of the glories of the Club until the bombing in the
Second World War necessitated removal into smaller premises, and the consequent dispersal of the larger portion
of it.

One of the major preoccupations of the General Committee during the first decade of the Club's existence was
difficulties with the staff. It is often stated that servants are
not what they were, but a perusal of the earlier annals of the
Carlton Club can but raise the problem, when were servants
what they were? Certainly not in the 'thirties of the nineteenth century, it would appear. A few examples will serve
to illustrate the truth of this, and to show the difference
between the unsatisfactory Club servants of those days and
the loyal and efficient service given by their successors in
more recent times.

On February 13th, 1833, we read in the committee minutes:
"A complaint being made that Cole the drawing-room
waiter had been tipsy and impertinent he was ordered to be
discharged and another servant procured in his place." On
March 19th, 1834: "Mr. FitzGerald attended to state a complaint he had to make of Wm. Frith the coffee-room waiter
for extreme insolence to himself in raising his voice and
answering in a very insolent manner. Mr. FitzGerald having
withdrawn: Resolved, That Wm. Frith be called in and informed that in consequence of his insolent behaviour to Mr.
FitzGerald he would be discharged at the end of the month
from the present date." On September 10th, 1836: "A letter

2. THE CARLTON CLUB IN 1932

from Col. Sibthorpe was read in which complaint was made of the Butler and Porter in the service of the Club having rode his horses. The matter investigated and admitted by the Butler and Porter. Resolved, That the Butler, as guilty of the impropriety and more especially as having (by demeaning himself in making himself the associate of an inferior servant of the establishment) disqualified himself for the situation he filled, be discharged and that the Porter be severely reprimanded for his misconduct."

That there was considerable slackness on the part of even the senior servants would seem to be proved by an incident which took place at a meeting of the committee on May 21st, 1834: "Charles Bolton the Hall Porter was called in and severely admonished and reprimanded upon the following complaint of his conduct:

I breakfasted at the Club on Wednesday last the 14th inst., and expected to find a note, making an appointment of some consequence. Upon enquiry of the Hall Porter, whom I told that I did expect such a note, I was assured no note had been left for me. At ten minutes before *twelve* the note was brought me, and I found it was dated *Tuesday evening* and appointed me to meet the writer at eleven Wednesday morning.

'Upon this I examined the Hall Porter particularly as to the time at which the note came, and I was assured most positively and repeatedly that it had been sent up the moment it arrived.'

I afterwards ascertained that it had been left at the Club the evening before, and the Hall Porter admitted the same afternoon that the statement he made in the morning was a wilful falsehood. Of course I should have thought nothing of the neglect; but I do not think I ought to pass over the lie, which until I had made enquiries elsewhere, was most obstinately adhered to.

Signed W. M. Praed.

In recent years there have been repeated complaints respec-

D

ting leakages of confidential information from the Club to the Press, but this is no new development, for very early in the Club's history there was an incident of this nature which occasioned the committee of the day considerable concern.

The matter was first brought up at a meeting on December 25th, 1833, when "A letter was read from Viscount Strangford[1] inclosing a copy of the *Satirist* newspaper of the 22nd inst. in which was inserted a paragraph detailing the proceedings of the Committee at their meeting of the 11th inst. Mr. Stone[2] was called in, and that portion of Lord Strangford's letter which related to him was read in his presence; and he was asked whether he adhered to the declaration made by him to Lord Strangford that he had only mentioned the proceedings of the Committee to the Clerk of the Kitchen and at his own table." Why Stone should have been suspected of the leakage is not clear, but on examination he adhered to his story "that the Clerk of the Kitchen and his own daughter were the only persons present, and that he had not mentioned the proceedings to any other persons whatever". As there were only three members of the committee present (which is hardly surprising in view of the fact that it was Christmas Day) it was decided to postpone discussion to a special meeting, and Stone was told "that he would do well in the meantime to make such enquiries as would lead to the discovery of the person who had furnished the details to the newspaper in question."

On January 15th, 1834, the matter came up again when "a

[1] The 6th Viscount. Born 1780, died 1855. He had a varied, but not very successful, diplomatic career, having been Minister in Portugal, Brazil, and Sweden, and Ambassador to Turkey and Russia. When he was sent on a special mission to Brazil in 1828, Greville wrote, "Lord Strangford to the Brazils, though the Duke knows as well as anybody that he cannot be trusted, and was recalled by Canning because he said and did all sorts of things at Constantinople for which he had no authority, and they found that no reliance whatever was to be placed in him."

[2] The Steward.

letter was read from Viscount Strangford enclosing a copy of the *Satirist* newspaper", though why a second copy should have been required is not easy to understand, and "the Secretary was requested to withdraw during the consideration of the contents of the letter". After further deliberation "the Steward was called in and informed that his situation and that of the Clerk of the Kitchen depended upon the discovery of the person who had furnished the *Satirist* with the details of the Committee".

The real inquest took place three days later.

The Committee proceeded to investigate further concerning the paragraph that appeared in the *Satirist* newspaper on the 22nd of December.

Mr. Jephson informed the Committee that the Clerk of the Kitchen had ascertained that the contents of the paragraph had been the subject of conversation at the bar of the St. Albans Hotel on the Thursday previous to its insertion in the *Satirist*, and that the subject had been mentioned to the two occasional waiters who attended the house dinner on that day.

The Clerk of the Kitchen was called in and examined. He stated that a person of the name of Messenger had spoken of the contents of the paragraph at the St. Albans Hotel, and it was communicated to him by a Mr. Lumley who was formerly cook to the late Duke of York, and also that the Steward had mentioned the circumstance at supper on Saturday the 14th to two occasional waiters and to others.

Mr. Stone was called in and examined upon the evidence given by the Clerk of the Kitchen. Mr. Stone acknowledged having mentioned the circumstance to the two occasional waiters at the supper table. Mr. Stone stated that the subject had been communicated by the cook to his friends out of the house and had become the subject of conversation in consequence.

Mr. Stone handed in the following letter addressed to the Editor of the *Satirist* which was read from the Chair:

Carlton House Terrace
January 17th, 1834

To the Editor of the *Satirist*

Sir,

There having appeared in your journal of the 22nd of December last and 5th of January of the present year under the head of "The Conservative Club" severe reflections and animadversions upon the conduct of the Committee for what you have designated an act of meanness in their refusing to allow certain items forming part of the weekly accounts submitted to their consideration; and it having been made a matter of charge against me by the Committee of such Establishment that I am the person who furnished the information upon which your remarks were grounded, I have to request you will do me the justice to state that I have never either directly or indirectly communicated with you, or any correspondent of yours, on the affairs of the Club, on any matter or subject connected therewith.

I am induced to trouble you with this letter in consequence of its having been intimated to me that unless I could procure an unqualified avowal from you that I am not the author or originator of the matter complained of my services as Steward to the Club would in future be dispensed with, the Committee having given me to understand that anyone who could be guilty of such a dereliction of duty as to disclose the result of their deliberations would be unworthy longer to remain an object of their patronage.

Signed, William Stone.

Delivered the 17th of January, 1834, a true copy of this letter to the *Satirist* office, Strand, directed to the Editor.

Signed, W. J. Bentham,
62 Piccadilly.

As was only to be expected, the Editor of the *Satirist* refused to divulge the source of his information, and the luckless Stone had to announce this fact to the committee at its next meeting, whereupon the following resolutions were passed:

The Committee having taken into its consideration the various circumstances connected with the publication of certain of their proceedings; are of opinion, that no proof has been elicited inculpating any individual of the Establishment of having communicated the proceedings of the Committee to the Press for the purpose of publication or of giving publicity to their proceedings with any malicious intent.

The Committee, however, in the exercise of the duty which devolves upon them, of selecting the servants of the Establishment according to their judgment of what may be most conducive to the general interests of the Club; are of opinion under all the circumstances of the case which has been brought before them, that it is not advisable to retain the House Steward, in consequence of his having committed such indiscretion as to render him unfit to remain in the service of the Club, and accordingly direct the usual notice of discharge be given him.

The Committee are also of opinion, that the character for which the House Steward may apply, should be given, in reference to his general conduct during the time he has been in the service of the Club.

Having passed these somewhat pompous resolutions the committee summoned Stone before them, and told him of their decision. Then "the Clerk of the Kitchen was called in and admonished that his conduct in talking of the proceedings of the Committee was very reprehensible, and should it occur again his services would be dispensed with". This was not, however, the end of the incident, for a letter was in due course received from Stone:

Feb. 17th, 1834

My Lords and Gentlemen,

The extremely painful situation in which I am placed by your decision, and the severe effect it must have upon my future prospects in life will I hope excuse the liberty I take in begging a reconsideration of the charge made against me. I am the more induced to solicit this indulgence because I think on further consideration, that the offensive paragraph will be found to contain matter which as I in the first instance remarked could not have been known to me for it will be in the recollection of the Honorable Committee, it was only at the close of the meeting that I was called in, therefore it must have been communicated by a person far better acquainted with the nature of the deliberations of the Committee than myself not having been present more than two or three minutes how could I have been aware that three of the Members severally rose and urged their objections, a statement which one of the Honorable Committee admitted to be correct.

This circumstance alone is materially corroborative of my innocence. I have endeavoured to discover the source through which the information was conveyed, but without effect, for the Editor of the *Satirist* told me, they never gave up the name of their correspondents, a very unfortunate custom for me as I feel convinced that the paragraph emanated from a party determined to injure me in your estimation in which unfortunately they have but too well succeeded.

Should, however, my further efforts be unavailing, with all respectful submission I beg to say that I feel it a duty I owe my family and myself to take such legal measures against the publisher of the paragraph as I may be advised to adopt.

Trusting your Lordships will be the kindness to pardon this intrusion on your valuable time.

I have the honour to be, etc.,

W. Stone.

No answer seems to have been made by the committee to this letter, and in July notification was received from a solicitor to the effect that Stone was about to commence an action against the *Satirist* to recover damages for the loss of his situation at the Carlton Club, and asking for a copy of the resolution discharging him from the Club's service. The committee were clearly alarmed at the possibility of becoming involved in the impending proceedings, and the secretary was instructed to say that "the copy of the resolution cannot be furnished; and further to add, that Mr. William Stone's dismissal was not in consequence of the Committee attributing the insertion in the *Satirist* paper of the paragraph in question to him; but in consequence of the impropriety of his conduct in talking of the proceedings of the Committee". With this the matter would seem to have dropped, for there is no further mention of Stone in the minutes: the whole incident throws an interesting light on the relations between the Club and its servants.

The committee's fear of publicity of any sort was evinced again early in the following year, for under date of April 28th, 1835, there is a minute to this effect:

A letter was read from Viscount Strangford calling the attention of the Committee to the great impropriety of communications being made to the public Press of the names of Members dining at the House Dinners. The names of the Members dining at the House Dinner on Thursday last having been published in the *Court Circular* and in several newspapers, and from its accuracy must have been supplied through some of the servants of the Club.

The Steward was called in and desired to caution all the servants as well as occasional waiters that communicating any intelligence of what passes in the Club to any newspaper would be upon pain of instant dismissal.

The members in these early days seem to have been a source of much less embarrassment to the committee than were the servants, though there were exceptions, and Lord

Ranelagh[1] seems to have been one of them to judge by a memorandum placed before the committee on July 19th, 1836:

The Secretary feels imperatively called on to bring under the notice of the Committee the conduct of Lord Viscount Ranelagh on Tuesday last in addressing most gross and abusive language to him for having in pursuance of his duty reported to the Committee on that day that his Lordship had not paid his annual subscription.

Lord Ranelagh became a supernumerary Member of the Club in 1834 being abroad, and was exempted from the payment of his subscription from that time until the 3rd of June last: on that day Lord Ranelagh first called at the Club, and in a day or two after the usual notice requiring the payment of the subscription was sent to his Lordship. The subscription not being paid within a fortnight a second notice was sent enclosing the Rules of the Club and requesting his Lordship's attention to the 10th Rule.

The subscription still remaining unpaid and no notice having been taken of the letters sent, the Secretary on the 12th July (a period of nearly six weeks having elapsed since Lord Ranelagh's return) in pursuance of his duty made known the circumstance to the Committee, who were of opinion that a letter should be immediately written to his Lordship calling for the payment. It was, however, upon further consideration agreed that some Member should acquaint his Lordship of the necessity for the immediate payment of his subscription, and it was ordered that if not paid on Tuesday the 19th that a final letter should be written acquainting his Lordship that if his subscription remained unpaid

---

[1] The 7th Viscount. Born 1812, died 1885. He had an adventurous youth, for after having served with the 1st Life Guards he fought for Don Carlos in the First Carlist War. In later life he was one of the protagonists of the Volunteer Movement. His name appeared in a trial, which aroused great interest in the summer of 1868, of a Madame Rachel, a vendor of cosmetics, for swindling a Mrs. Borradaile, on pretence that Lord Ranelagh, who was an occasional visitor to Madame Rachel's shop in New Bond Street, was in love with her, and that in order to become the wife of a nobleman she must be enamelled and "made beautiful for ever" at a cost of £1,000. Lord Ranelagh swore he knew nothing of the matter, and Madame Rachel was sentenced to five years' penal servitude.

on the Tuesday following his name would be erased from the List of Members.

Immediately after the Committee had adjourned on Tuesday last, Lord Ranelagh entered the Secretary's office, left the door open after him, and in a high tone of voice, and in a most insulting manner, made use of the following language as nearly as possible.

"I say, Mr. Jephson, what do you mean by reporting me to the Committee for not paying my subscription? It was a damned piece of impertinence on your part. It was a damned impertinent thing of you, and you had no right to do it; and I consider you a damned impertinent fellow for doing it. So, Sir, because I do not happen to have money about me I am to be reported for non-payment of my subscription. I repeat, Sir, you are a damned impertinent fellow for having made any such report." Lord Ranelagh addressed much more to the same effect. The Secretary made no reply whatever, but that he had acted in pursuance of his duty in reporting the non-payment of all subscriptions to the Managing Committee.

Under these circumstances of gross insult offered to him by a Member of the Club, the Secretary (feeling that he is but the organ of the Committee) deems it to be his bounden duty to lay the matter fully before that body, under the firm hope and conviction that they will not allow their officer in the discharge of a disagreeable but a most necessary part of his duty to be subjected to such unprovoked insult, or outraged by such gross and ungentlemanlike language as that addressed to him by Lord Ranelagh. The Secretary cannot doubt but that the Committee will in vindication of their orders, carried into execution by their officer, see such reparation made to him as they shall consider warranted by the occasion, and in this hope the Secretary throws himself entirely upon the protection of the Committee.

What steps were then taken to bring home to Lord Ranelagh the enormity of his offence we do not know, but something was clearly done, for there is a further minute on the subject on July 26th:

A letter was read from Lord Ranelagh expressing his regret for having made use of any expressions on the 12th July last which were deemed offensive and insulting by the Secretary, and requesting to withdraw them. The Committee were of opinion that the letter was sufficiently satisfactory, and the Secretary expressed himself to the same effect.

Jephson would thus appear to have been of a singularly forgiving nature, and Ranelagh seems to have got off more easily than his behaviour deserved: presumably he also paid his subscription, but of that there is no record.

By the earliest rules the membership was tentatively fixed at 700, but in 1833 it was raised to 800. We have Disraeli's evidence, quoted above, for the large number of candidates coming forward, and it was primarily to relieve the heavy waiting list that the new premises were built in the 'fifties. In 1857 the number was increased to 900, and during the ensuing seventy years it was raised on several occasions until by the time that the Club celebrated its centenary in 1932 the figure stood at 1,850, comprising Peers, Heirs Apparent, and Members of the House of Commons, and 1,360 ordinary members. The subscription did not increase anything like so rapidly, for when the Club was founded it was fixed at 10 guineas, and on the outbreak of the Second World War it was only 17: in the same period the entrance fee rose from 10 guineas to £40.

It is not uninteresting to look at some of the prices paid during the early years of the Club's existence. In March 1833, it was paying 5s. 6d. a pound for Souchong, and 8s. a pound for Hyson, tea "procured from the India House". In October of the same year the committee ordered Wallsend coal at the price of 22s. a ton, but by August 1837, the cost had risen to 27s. As for wine, soon after the Club's foundation the committee gave instructions that "the Club shall purchase so much as shall be necessary for the present consumption if the quality shall appear good, and the purchase can be made at a price not very exorbitant". How this was translated into action can be seen by a minute of May 15th, 1833:

Mr. Robert Cockburn of Leith submitted a proposal by letter to supply the Club with wines at fixed prices upon certain terms (letter addressed to Lord Strangford). The Committee decided to give Mr. Cockburn an order, and directed a letter to be written to Lord Strangford to order:
One HH-d of Claret at 84/6 a dozen,
Half a pipe of Port at 50/- a dozen,
upon the terms contained in Mr. Cockburn's letter. . . . The Steward was directed to procure some table ale from a person who supplies the House of Commons.

The committee's choice of wine did not, however, always meet with the approval of the members, as the following entry on July 16th, 1839, proves:

Mr. R. Hodgson's dinner bill of the 13th inst. with his remarks regarding Gardiner's Sherry on the back of it was laid before the Committee who drew up the following letter which was ordered to be sent to Mr. Hodgson:
"I am directed by the Committee to inform you that your complaint on the 13th July as follows was laid before them this day, 'Gardiner's Sherry only fit for the Servants' Hall. I beg to recommend the use of some drinkable Sherry in the Coffee Room'. The Committee desire me to express their regret that the complaint is so worded that they must decline to entertain it."

Another item of interest is the wages paid to the Club's servants, though the surviving evidence on this point is scanty. On January 30th, 1833, "Louis Loyer was hired as cook at £200 a year to include his aid", the last word being a curious, almost American, way of describing his assistant.

Loyer did not, however, continue long in the Club's employ for he was dismissed at the beginning of the following July on account of "having upon various occasions absented himself from his duty without leave, and having hired himself out to dress a dinner yesterday when his services were required in the Club". His place was filled temporarily, for it was not until January 29th, 1834, that "Monsieur Lozeron was engaged as head cook at 3½ guineas per week for six months certain, if by the year at £140". The successor of the unfortunate Stone as steward received £160 per annum.

Further particulars appear in the minutes of January 24th, 1837, when it was stated: "The Committee engaged Mr. Williams as Head Cook at £150, and Monsieur Louis as second cook at £70 per annum. Several applications for the situation of Butler were gone into, and James Webb appearing to be the most eligible one for the Club to engage he was accordingly hired at £70 per annum". The female staff – still-room maids, housemaids, and the like – seem to have received between £12 and £20 a year, and these wages included full board and lodging. From time to time a cash bonus was given to, at any rate, the senior servants.

As regards what may be described as the general financing of the Club no great difficulty seems to have been experienced by the committee, and on March 5th, 1834, it recommended "a floating balance of not less than £2,000 should be kept at the Bankers' to remunerate them for the trouble and expense of managing the account". The building of the first club house was financed by a loan from the Hon. Sidney Herbert,[1] M.P., secured by a mortgage.

---

[1] Born 1810, died 1861. M.P. for South Wilts. While he was Secretary for War he sent Florence Nightingale to Constantinople. In 1860 he was created Baron Herbert of Lea.

The ordinary amenities were not as great as a later generation of members would have required, and very precise
instructions were, for instance, laid down in respect of the
number of members allowed to dine in the Club at any one
time, presumably on account of the limited accommodation
available. Members could only dine if they formed a party of
not less than six or more than fourteen by giving notice not
later than midday. The charge for dinner was 15s, exclusive
of wine, and if a member who had put down his name failed
to dine a fine of 10s. 6d. was imposed.

One or two extracts from the committee minutes will
serve to give an idea of the habits of the members of those
days. On May 23rd, 1832, it was ordered that "on all days
except Saturday and Sunday a joint to be ready at 4 o'clock
during the sitting of Parliament"; also that "the charge of
each table be one shilling which includes bread, butter,
cheese, English pickles, small beer, and biscuits". On February 13th of the following year "Suppers were directed to be
provided after ten o'clock at night on Mondays, Tuesdays,
Thursdays, and Fridays at 4 shillings a head exclusive of
wines, liqueurs, soda water, etc."; while a later direction was
to the effect that these "suppers were to be ready consisting
of hot soup, cold meats, salad, oysters, and any pastry ready,
the charge for each person to be 2s. 6d. If orders are sent for a
better supper each person to be charged 4s.". The price of
breakfast was, in February 1836, fixed at 1s. 6d. to include
two eggs. Lunch was, of course, an unknown meal at this
time.

It is to be observed that there is no mention in the rules of
the admission of guests into the Club, but they were clearly
not allowed, and the reason why they were not mentioned
may well be that at that time it was not customary for guests

to be admitted to any club. The first reference to them occurs in the minutes of November 7th, 1837, when "the Committee decided to illuminate on the 9th inst. on the occasion of Her Majesty's going to the City, and also that Members should introduce ladies and children to the Club House to view the procession, but that no Gentlemen not being Members of the Club were to be admitted". The precedent thus created was rigidly adhered to even after the First World War when female guests were admitted on the night of a general election, but save on a few very special occasions no man who was not a member entered the Club until it moved to Arthur's old premises at 69 St. James's Street.

The vexed question of smoking made its appearance very early in the Club's history, for on February 23rd, 1836, the committee "directed a notice to be put up in the Morning Room that there being a smoking-room, smoking could not be allowed in any other apartment". Before long, however, a further concession would appear to have been made to the smokers, for in the article in the *Illustrated Times* of March 15th, 1856, to which allusion has already been made there occurs the passage: "Hark! what is that noise that makes little Lord Tofts look up from Paul de Kock? It is the rattle of billiard balls from the adjoining billiard-room, where a Scotch and an Irish member are preparing themselves for their silent votes to-night. This is a billiard-room where no smoking is allowed; if we go up another flight of stairs, we shall find one where no such restriction is imposed, and where the balls can scarcely be seen for smoke." The contest between the smokers and the non-smokers continued for the next seventy years, and the smokers gradually gained ground as one room after another was opened to them. By the outbreak of the Second World War the only rooms in which smoking was prohibited were the coffee-room and the small library. At 69 St. James's Street the coffee-room alone is barred to the smokers.

Billiards seems to have been more popular in the early days of the Club than it was subsequently to become, for on March 1st, 1836, the committee "directed that the Marker for the Billiard room should be in attendance every day except on Sundays until one o'clock in the morning, at which hour he should be allowed to retire". The twentieth century witnessed a decline in the interest in the game, though two tables were in existence until the Club was bombed; for a while there was one at 69 St. James's Street, but it was abolished consequent upon the alterations made to enable the annexe to re-open in 1952.

By 1840 it may be said that the Club was fully established, and had already acquired a position of influence and importance in the social and political life of London; that it had done so in such short space of time was in no small measure due to the ability and energy of those who were responsible for its management.

CHAPTER II

The Club in Politics

EADERS of *Phineas Finn* will remember that when that hero was elected as Liberal M.P. for Loughshane his creator, Anthony Trollope, attributed to one of the Dublin Conservative papers the observation that "it was all the fault of the Carlton Club in not sending a proper candidate". *Phineas Finn* is admittedly a work of fiction, but Trollope was far too good a political novelist to attribute functions to the Club which it did not exercise, and there can, in fact, be no doubt that during the first fifty years of its existence it played to a large extent the part now performed by the Conservative Central Office.

It is obvious that from the very beginning there was a clearly-marked distinction between the social and political activities of the Club as the following quotations from the minutes prove:

21.II.1837.
A letter read from Mr. J. Walker Ord requesting an advance of funds from the Committee to carry on the Metropolitan Conservative Journals. An answer was directed to be sent to Mr. Ord that the Committee regret they cannot appropriate the funds of the Club to such a purpose.

18.IV.1837.
A letter was read from Mr. Nichols addressed to the Secretary requesting an interview upon the subject of an election for the

3. THE MORNING ROOM OF THE PRESENT CARLTON CLUB

Tower Hamlets, which was referred to Mr. Bonham[1] and Mr. Ross.

23.I.1844.

A letter was read from Mr. Cockton requesting to know if the Committee would aid him in establishing a Conservative newspaper in Bury St. Edmund's; an answer was directed to be sent stating that the Committee had no funds belonging to the Club which could be appropriated to such a purpose.

These are the only references in the earlier minutes of the committee to any proposed political activity outside the walls of the Club, and there is no mention whatsoever of the Political Committee at a time when its influence throughout the kingdom was very considerable indeed. Whether this Political Committee never kept any minutes, or whether they have been lost, is impossible to say, but the fact remains that to discover what was done – and how it was done – one must go to other authorities than the surviving Club records, at any rate until the period immediately preceding the First World War.

Ostrogorski, in his authoritative work *Democracy and the Organization of Political Parties*, leaves his readers under no illusion as to the importance of the Carlton in the middle of the nineteenth century. "The period which immediately succeeded the Reform Bill", he says, "was also marked by the appearance of central party organizations, the influence and activity of which were destined to radiate from London over the whole country. The first of them was the Carlton Club, founded by the Conservatives . . . which was intended to combine the purpose of a social club and of a centre for rallying the party and for political action in general".

He then continues:

[1] Francis Robert Bonham, M.P., the Conservative Chief Whip.

The plan of the Club succeeded. Members of Parliament belonging to both Houses, from the leaders down to the most obscure members, met at the Carlton, laid their heads together there, and gave or received the word of command. The local leaders, the provincial notables who came up to London and wished to see the great men of the party, were sure to find them at the Carlton, and there they could approach them on a footing of equality and even of intimacy. The relations to which this gave rise and the influences resulting therefrom linked the constituencies to the Carlton all the more strongly because the tie was invisible. The note struck at the Carlton Club was invariably and faithfully re-echoed in the country, because there too, in every locality, the local leaders and mass of electors were united by the same imperceptible ties of social influences. A political committee formed in the club itself kept up constant relations with the local associations or agents, and stimulated the work of electoral registration. The Liberals were not long in discerning the part played by the Carlton Club, and about 1836 they founded a similar institution with the name of the Reform Club, which in its turn soon became the headquarters of the Liberal Party. It also had its political committee, which discharged the same duties as that of the Carlton.

The controlling influence in the political activities of the Club was the Chief Whip, whose authority was not confined to the walls of the House of Commons as was subsequently to be the case. It is true that he could no longer traffic in seats as had been the case in the earlier years of the century, but what has been described as "a sort of electoral labour exchange" grew up in the Carlton. After the Tory defeat in 1832 Conservative associations had, largely owing to the efforts of Sir Robert Peel, come into existence in various parts of the country with, later, a Central Association to co-ordinate their activities; and in due course there was set up a Conservative Central Office. All these bodies at first worked in close harmony with the Carlton, which was the head-quarters of the Whips.

To quote Ostrogorski again:

Besides the management of registration and of the outvoters the Association also undertook the recommendation of Parliamentary candidates. Men who wished to stand for Parliament applied to the Association. The Whip took note of their political opinions, if they had any, and especially of the pecuniary sacrifices which they were disposed to make for the electoral struggle. He entered them in the candidates' book and classed them. A good Whip, after a talk with a candidate, could see at once whether he would do for any constituency, and fixed on the constituency which would probably suit him. Then, when there was an application for a candidate, the Association sent down a name to its local agent. The agent, who was frequently the secretary of the Registration Society, called a meeting of the party leaders, the most influential men, and submitted the candidate's name to them. Very often a deputation came up to London, and an interview was arranged between it and the candidate in the office of the Association. If they did not come to terms, the Association offered another candidate; it always had a supply of all shades of opinion and suited to all tastes. The Association did not put pressure on the constituencies in the choice of candidates, it only acted the part of honest broker. The Association did not spend any money on the elections, it was the candidate who had to defray all the expense. If he was a poor man and if his presence in Parliament was desirable in the interests of the party, the Whips supplied him with money; they had funds subscribed by the wealthy men of the party which they used at their discretion. That a portion of these funds was employed in bribing voters when the candidate was not rich enough to do it himself, is not improbable.

The Conservative organization may thus be said to have had a trinitarian basis. First of all there were the Whips who worked with and through the Political Committee of the Club; their power at Westminster was slight compared with what it is today, but elsewhere it was most formidable, and they exercised functions which have long passed to the Central Office. Next came the Central Association which was in touch with the local associations through what were termed correspondents, but would now be described as secretaries. Lastly, there was the nascent Central Office, which kept in close contact with the Club, of which the leading Conservatives, both in and out of Parliament, were members.

In contrast with the conditions of a later age the aspirants to Parliamentary honours were relatively few, and they came from the class which used the Club. It has already been shown how vital Disraeli regarded membership of the Carlton to be to the advancement of his political ambitions, and he was no exception. Thus it was comparatively easy for the Whips to become personally acquainted with potential candidates, and to form a fair estimate both of their aspirations and of their abilities. Furthermore, it must be remembered that in those days there was very little political activity in the constituencies between elections. There were no paid agents whose duty it was ever to keep party politics to the fore. The local correspondents of the Central Association were generally solicitors; they were not paid for their services, but it was to their interest to render them, and that for two reasons. Their activity on behalf of the Party was liable to increase their private practice owing to the number of people with whom it brought them into contact, and it also marked them out in advance for appointment as election agents, who conducted the election campaign for the candidate. This was a very lucrative occupation, for in addition to the remuneration received directly, the agent could make a good deal out of the election expenses which all passed through his hands and which often amounted to a very considerable sum.

"The intervention from London", wrote Ostrogorski, "haunted people's minds in the provinces, even when it never took place; and, in accordance with the old tradition, it was attributed to the Carlton Club." In effect, the Club, like the Conservative Central Office in more recent times, was often credited with a mysterious, and even sinister, influence behind the scenes both in London and in the provinces: when candidates did well, they were quite ready to attribute their success to their own superior merits; but when they did badly, then they were only too willing to blame the Club and its Political Committee. What cannot, however, be questioned is that the Carlton was for a number of years a very effective force in the world of British politics.

Soon after the middle of the century a definite modification began in the relative values of the three main forces in the Conservative organization; there were several reasons for this, of which the most important was the growth of the popular element in the Party. However successful the Carlton might be in its political activities it could only bring together members of the upper and middle classes, but after the Reform Act of 1867 these classes represented but a small minority of political society. The extension of the franchise had brought into existence the Conservative working-man, and he soon began to make his weight felt in the local associations. It is true that the change in this respect proceeded but slowly, and for some years the annual meetings of the National Union of Constitutional and Conservative Associations were marked by a dullness and an insignificance which gave little evidence of any real vitality. The machinery, however, was there, and it only awaited the coming of a man who knew how to make it work.

Nor was this all, for the position of the Chief Whip was

becoming very different from what it had been in the
'thirties and 'forties. As party distinctions were more sharply
drawn so party discipline in the House of Commons became
stricter, and this imposed added responsibilities on the Whips,
who, in consequence, tended to concentrate to an increasing
extent upon their duties at Westminster; this naturally gave
them less time to concern themselves with candidates and
with the constituencies, and this side of their work gradually
passed to the Central Office, which had its own staff and
premises, and did not operate through the Political Committee of the Carlton. As has been said, all these changes took
place slowly, and it was not until the political crises of the
'eighties that the new balance of forces in the Party became
manifest.

Disraeli had been by no means unaware of what was in
progress, and while he was in Opposition in the early 'seventies he had been quietly working at Conservative reorganization; the result of his labours was the machine which did so
much to bring him victory at the General Election of 1874.
After the defeat of 1868 a special *ad hoc* committee had been
set up to investigate the causes of what had taken place, but
it was soon evident that this was not enough. "An entirely
new system must be set up; and Disraeli looked about for a
young and ambitious Conservative who would be ready to
devote the best years of his life to working out such a scheme.
His choice fell upon John Eldon Gorst[1], a barrister who had
had a distinguished career at Cambridge, and had sat for a
year or two in Parliament, but was now no longer a member."[2]
At the same time Disraeli paid constant personal attention to

[1] Born 1835, died 1916. Later a member of the Fourth Party, Solicitor-General,
and Under-Secretary for India. He left the Conservative Party on the question of
Tariff Reform, and in 1910 contested Preston as a Liberal, but was defeated.
[2] Buckle, G. E.: *The Life of Benjamin Disraeli, Earl of Beaconsfield*, vol. V, p. 184 .

all that was being done, and he was always ready to give Gorst the benefit of his sagacity and experience at every stage. Writing to a friend in October 1873 he mentioned that "after every borough election, an expert visits the scene of action, and prepares a confidential despatch for me, that, so far as is possible, I may be thoroughly acquainted with the facts".

The somewhat unexpected reversal of fortune in 1880 called for another special investigation, and Sir Winston Churchill has thus analysed the situation in his biography of his father, Lord Randolph:

After the electoral disaster of 1880 a meeting had been held at Bridgewater House, under the auspices of Lord Beaconsfield, to examine the causes of defeat. A committee, formed chiefly of Members of the Carlton Club, had been appointed to consider various methods of reforming, popularizing and improving the Party organization. This committee was never dissolved. It continued to exist, and under the title of the "Central Committee" assumed the direction and management of all Party affairs and controlled the large funds subscribed for Party purposes. The National Union of Conservative Associations, upon the other hand, was a body formed on a basis of popular representation. Its branches had spread all over the country and its membership included many of the more active local leaders of the Conservative Party in the great towns. It was, however, deprived of all share in Party government by the Central Committee and jealously excluded from possessing any financial independence.

Lord Randolph was just beginning his campaign for Tory Democracy, but he had first of all to convert his own party to his views, and the National Union of Conservative Associations seemed to be a weapon admirably designed for his purpose. These tactics might in the long run make for power, but they were not calculated to enhance Lord Randolph's popularity, as his son has freely admitted:

Nothing but Lord Randolph Churchill's undisputed predominance in debate and his unequalled popularity in the country could have sustained him against the forces which he had determined to engage. From one motive or another, from conscientious and perfectly intelligible distrust, from vulgar jealousy, from respect for discipline and authority, from a dull resentment at the disturbance he created, nearly all the most influential Conservatives in the House of Commons and the Carlton Club were leagued against him. Lord Salisbury was hostile to him. Sir Stafford Northcote had good reason to be so. All the old men who had sat in the late Cabinet, were alarmed; all the new men who hoped to sit in the next, were envious of his surprising rise to power. Scarcely a name can be mentioned of those who had held office in the past or were to hold it in the future, which was not at this time arrayed against him. And with all of them he was now to come into violent collision.

Into the details of the ensuing struggle it is unnecessary to enter here for they belong to the history of the Conservative Party rather than to that of the Carlton Club. In due course Churchill was elected Chairman of the National Union, and waged a strenuous campaign against the Central Committee; finally a compromise was reached between him and Lord Salisbury in 1884, by the terms of which the Central Committee was dissolved, and the powers of the National Union were greatly increased. From that date it may be said that the *rôle* of the Club as an important factor in the Conservative organization came to an end. It continued, through the Political Committee, to play its part, but it never again possessed the power which it had wielded in the middle of the century.

Lord Randolph Churchill was, however, soon to have a more pleasant recollection of the Club than that inspired by his opposition to its dominance in the organization of the Party. After the Liberal defeat at the General Election of 1886 Salisbury was called upon to form a government. He "accepted the commission", Sir Winston Churchill writes, "with leave to resign it, if necessary, to Lord Hartington. Forthwith he strongly pressed the leader of the Whigs to form a government and assured him, if he did so, of Conservative support. Lord Hartington knew that any government he could form, would be practically Conservative in its composition, and must be called by that name. He believed that in these circumstances the Liberal Unionist Party would dissolve, Mr. Chamberlain and the Radical section splitting off and probably rejoining the Liberals. He therefore declined."

Salisbury called a Party meeting at the Carlton, explained the position, and announced his intention of forming a purely Conservative ministry. Before leaving the Club he sent for Hicks-Beach and Churchill. "I declined", wrote Sir Michael in later years, "to continue Leader of the House of Commons. I felt that Lord Randolph Churchill was superior in eloquence, ability and influence to myself; that the position of leader in name, but not in fact, would be intolerable; and that it was better for the Party and the country that the leader in fact should be also leader in name. Lord Salisbury very strongly pressed me to remain, saying that character was of most importance, and quoting Lord Althorp as an instance; but I insisted. I had very great difficulty in persuading Lord Randolph to agree. I spent more than half an hour with him in the committee room of the Carlton before I could persuade him, and I was much struck by the hesitation he showed on account of what he said was his youth and inexperience in taking the position. He insisted on my going to Ireland, pointing out that I could only honourably give up the leadership by taking what was at the moment the most difficult position in the government." Thus it was in the Carlton, to all intents and purposes, that Lord Randolph Churchill at the age of thirty-seven became Chancellor of the Exchequer and Leader of the House of Commons.

So much for the Club in politics during the earlier part of the Victorian era, but what of politics in the Club? To what extent were the repercussions of events outside its walls felt inside the Carlton? The question is not an easy one to answer owing to the paucity of evidence, but there are a number of indications which serve as straws to show which way the wind was blowing at various times.

First of all, however, it must be appreciated that, for reasons which have been discussed above, the Club was a great deal more of a political centre than has been the case of more recent years. To no inconsiderable extent it filled the *rôle* of the smoking room of the House of Commons at the present time. At any rate since the Second World War a considerable proportion of the Club's members have used it as a restaurant rather than as a club: they go in for the purpose of eating and drinking, and when they have eaten and drunk they return to their offices and their homes. They do not visit the Club for the purpose of talking politics as their predecessors did, nor are they, for the most part, what their predecessors were, namely the people who carry weight in politics, although of course, most members of the Cabinet are members of the Club. Unless this difference in background is understood the distinction between the political atmosphere of the Carlton in the mid-nineteenth and mid-twentieth century cannot be appreciated.

Not for the last time in the Club's history the question of Protection and Free Trade divided its members before it had been ten years in existence. As early as April 7th, 1840, the committee was made officially aware of the division which existed on the subject:

The following letter addressed to the Committee, signed by the Duke of Buckingham[1] and several Members of the Club was read:

To the Committee. We beg leave to call the attention of the Committee to the following circumstance. A House dinner took place on Monday the 30th of March last composed of 60 Members of the Club chiefly representing agricultural constituencies. It was there unanimously agreed on to call together the Members of the Club favorable to the principle of protection to agriculture on the following Saturday with a view to counteract the efforts of the Anti-Corn Law League, and a notice was placed on the chimney-piece of the reading-room to that effect. This notice was withdrawn by some person on the morning of Saturday on which the meeting was to have taken place, consequently many Members of the Club who would have been present did not attend, and the object of those who represented agricultural districts was in a great measure frustrated. We therefore request the Committee to institute an enquiry that it may be known by whose authority the notice was withdrawn which was posted in the reading-room from the 31st of March till Saturday the 4th of April.

The committee had, in fact, already made up its mind to walk warily, and whatever might be the private opinions of those who composed it they decided that members should be free to hold and express any views they liked on the question of tariffs. Incidentally, it is not uninteresting to note that when, in 1886, the Liberal Party was split over Home Rule the committees of Brooks's and the Reform Club followed the precedent set forty years earlier by the Carlton.

[1] The 2nd Duke of the Grenville creation. Born 1787, died 1861. Lord Privy Seal, 1841–42. By a system of accumulating estates purchased with borrowed money, and by excessive expenditure, he became a ruined man within eight years of his succession to the title in 1839. He is one of the few dukes to have died at the Great Western Hotel, Paddington.

Lord Redesdale[1] was in the chair when the Duke of Buckingham's letter was read, and he was deputed to reply to it, which he did in the following terms:

As Chairman of the Committee this day, I am directed by them to reply to the letter addressed to them by Your Grace and several other Members of the Club, on the subject of a notice for a meeting of the Members favorable to agricultural protection having been removed from the morning-room. If you attended the Committee last year at the time when a meeting was held on Irish Railways you will recollect that the inconvenience of such meetings was unanimously assented to, and that a communication was made from the Committee to the parties who were instrumental in calling it, which led to another meeting on the same subject of which notice had been given being abandoned. It has always been considered that notices ought not to be put up without the sanction of the Committee; at the present moment a notice respecting the subscription to the statue of the Duke of Wellington in Edinburgh is on the chimney-piece, but even for such an object, of which there cannot be two opinions in the Club, the permission of the Committee was first obtained and is affixed to the notice.

Such being the practice of the Club and the decision of the Committee of last year, when my attention was called to the notice in question by some Members connected with the manufacturing districts who were exceedingly hurt at what they considered a Club Meeting being called on such a subject which they deemed injurious to their interests with their constituencies, I myself as a Member of the Committee removed the notice which I considered irregular. As it was not signed I did not feel myself called upon to communicate my reasons for so doing to anyone as I should in courtesy have done had I known anyone who took a personal interest in the notice.

[1] The 1st Earl. Born 1805, died 1886. Chairman of Committees and Deputy Speaker of the House of Lords, 1851–86. Disraeli wrote of him that "he has many excellent qualities and talents, but . . . is narrowminded, prejudiced, and utterly unconscious of what is going on in the country, its wishes, opinions, and feelings". He gave an annual dinner to the peers at Greenwich, and to the end of his life he wore the old-fashioned tail-coat and brass buttons of an earlier generation.

I believe you would have thanked me for removing a notice for the abolition of the Corn Laws, and you must of course admit that any Member might put up such a notice if he pleased should the other be deemed regular. I trust you will on consideration see that such counter-proceedings would be most injurious to the Club, and that it is a most wholesome rule that such meetings should be declared irregular. I need hardly add, that I had not the slightest intention of giving offence to anyone, and I beg you will be kind enough to communicate this to the other Members of the Club who signed the letter to the Committee.

As I am personally a strong supporter of the existing Corn Laws I trust that you and all will be convinced that I was influenced by no other motives than the good of the Club and the maintenance of the regulations of the Committee in removing the notice.

A fortnight later instructions were given for the following notice to be put up in the morning room:

The attention of the Committee has been called to the serious inconvenience which may arise from notices for meetings to be held at the Club being placed by Members in the morning room.

To private meetings for political or other purposes of Members assembling by mutual agreement at the Club there can be no objection, but when notices are publicly placed in the rooms the assembly takes in a great degree the character of a Club Meeting, and the objects there advocated may be represented out of doors as those to which Members are considered to be pledged. This may lead to counter notices being issued to remove such impressions, the posting of which might cause much ill feeling and injury to the Club.

The Committee feel it to be their duty to check all proceedings which may be in the slightest degree disagreeable to either the majority or minority of the Members, and especially when they are of a character which may render the continuance of individuals as Members of the Club inconvenient in reference to the opinions which may be entertained by their constituents of the obligations imposed upon them by their connexions with the Club.

No notice therefore in future can be allowed to remain posted in the rooms which has not received the sanction of the Committee.

It has also been represented to the Committee that much inconvenience has arisen from notices being improperly placed on the Parliamentary notice-board. The only persons authorized by the Committee to post those notices are Lord Redesdale, Sir George Clerk, M.P., Sir Thomas Fremantle, M.P., Mr. Henry Baring, M.P.

As will be seen, the committee adhered to this impartial attitude throughout the crisis caused by Peel's abandonment of Protection, and their example was followed by their successors in the following century when there were differences in the Party, first on the question of tariffs, and later in connection with self-government in India. Successive committees have set their face against anything that savoured of heresy-hunting. All the same, divisions in the Party were a cause of concern, and on June 1st, 1840, Sir James Graham, soon to be Home Secretary, wrote to Charles Arbuthnot, "There is also a new club to be formed, an off-shoot from the Carlton, from which I anticipate great mischief and a serious schism in the Conservative ranks. All this is most unfortunate, when we are on the verge of success and when at any moment our victory may be decisive." The new club was the Conservative.

The Party was certainly "on the verge of success", for at the General Election in the summer of 1841 it obtained a majority of seventy. The Conservative triumph, however, was to be short-lived, for in January 1846 Peel announced his measures to establish Free Trade, which in due course became law, and in the following June the Protectionists had their revenge by voting with the Opposition on a Coercion Bill, which put ministers in a minority. For the next six years the country was governed by what proved to be the last Whig administration, under Lord John Russell, and then there was the Conservative ministry of Lord Derby which on December 18th, 1852, was defeated by the combined vote of the Whigs and the Peelites.

The repercussion of these events in the Club must have been considerable, and the surviving evidence goes to prove that tempers became heated on more than one occasion. For example, on February 17th, 1846, just after Peel had announced his fiscal proposals, the secretary called the attention of the committee to the fact that the Prime Minister's name had been struck out of one of the printed lists of members lying on a table in the morning room, and the word "withdrawn" written against it; whereupon the committee somewhat sententiously placed it upon record that "such a proceeding on the part of any member of the Club is unwarrantable, and should it occur again will require public notice."

Relations between the Peelites and the orthodox Conservatives steadily deteriorated, and during the last weeks of the Derby administration the following correspondence passed between the committee and the Marquess of Downshire:

12.X.1852.

The following letter was read from the Marquess of Downshire[1]:

[1] The 4th Marquess. Born 1812, died 1868. He possessed immense physical strength, and is said, when a boy at Eton, to have killed a bargee by a blow of his fist. One contemporary described him as "a quite gentlemanlike man", but Jane Carlyle called him in later life "a dear, good, kind-hearted savage of a man".

Hillsborough
October 6th, 1852

Sir,

I shall be obliged to you to inform me if it is the intention of
the Committee of the Carlton Club to take any steps to remove
Members from the Club who now hold and have for some time
held opinions opposed to those which qualified them for election.
I for one have felt much annoyance from seeing these Gentlemen
I allude to constant frequenters of your Club, and I know that my
feeling is the same as that of many other Members. I should have
written to you before, but was told by a friend that an influential
Member of the Committee gave as his opinion that after the
election the good feeling of these Gentlemen would perhaps
induce them to withdraw.

The elections are now over, and I wish to know if this feeling
has come out, or if the Committee mean to wait for its spontaneous appearance.

I remain, Sir,
Your obt, Sevt.
Downshire.

To the Secretary
   of the Carlton Club

You will have the kindness to refer this note to the chairman
of the next meeting of Committee, and to no other.

Ordered that the following letter be addressed to the Marquess
of Downshire:

Carlton Club
October 12th, 1852.

My Lord,

I am directed in reply to the enquiry in your Lordship's letter
of the 6th inst as to whether "it is the intention of the Committee
of the Carlton Club to take any steps to remove Members from
the Club who now hold opinions opposed to those which qualified them for election", to state that the subject has not been discussed in the Committee of Management, and, in reply to your
Lordship's further enquiry as to whether any withdrawals from

the Club have recently taken place, I beg to say there have not been any.

I am, My Lord,

respectfully,

Your Lordship's most obed^t.

and Hb^{le} Servant

W. Rainger,

Secretary.

15.X.1852.

The following letter from the Marquess of Downshire was laid upon the table:

Hillsborough

October 15, 52.

Sir,

I beg to acknowledge the receipt of your letter of the 13th inst.

Finding from it that no steps are being taken by the Committee to preserve the political character of the Carlton Club, and to prevent its being what it is now, a mixed society of Peelites, Radicals, Whigs, and Tories, I beg to inform you that I shall withdraw my name from the list of its Members, and I request you to erase my name from your books after the 31st December, 1852.

I remain, Sir,

Your obed^t Sev^t

Downshire.

The committee was thus adhering to its resolution not to engage in heresy-hunting, but feeling began to run very high indeed when the Peelites assisted in the overthrow of the Derby administration, and it clearly reached fever-heat when it became known that Gladstone was about to take office as Chancellor of the Exchequer in the coalition government of Lord Aberdeen. In this connection the following extract from *The Sunday Times* of December 26th, 1852, speaks for itself:

A scene took place at the Carlton Club on Monday evening which has excited much attention, and may yet lead to very unpleasant consequences. While Mr. Gladstone was reading a newspaper certain Tory members of the House of Commons came into the room, and employed extremely insulting language to the Right Hon. gentleman, telling him among other things that he had no right to belong to a Conservative Club, but ought to be pitched out of the window in the direction of the Reform Club. Mr. Gladstone addressed the parties in the most courteous terms, but they repeated their insulting language, ordered candles in another room, and then left Mr. Gladstone alone.

In spite of the provocation he had received, Gladstone does not appear to have brought the incident to the notice of the committee, and he did not resign from the Club until 1860 when he had already been for eight months Chancellor of the Exchequer in the Liberal government of Lord Palmerston. Even then the severance of his connection with the Carlton was a trifle irregular, for on March 27th, 1860, it was ordered by the committee that "the Secretary be directed to address a letter to the Right Hon. W. E. Gladstone, M.P., to inform him that the sum of £10–10–0 is due from him to the funds of the Club in consequence of his notice of withdrawal not being given previous to the 1st day of January."

This provoked the following reply:

Downing Street
March 29th, 60

Sir,

The note which you have had the goodness to send me is precisely that under which I formed the intention last year to retire from the Carlton Club, and the note I addressed to you, drawn forth by your own to me, was intended to signify the same instruction, and my consent to the erasure of my name. I was not aware that under those circumstances it was usual to require payment of the subscription from Members thus withdrawing. But if I understand from you that my name has not been permitted to remain on the list of Members since the date of my note, or if I learn that in the judgment of the Committee I have notwithstanding what I have stated above inadvertently made myself liable, I will at once forward the sum required.

It is, I hope, hardly necessary for me to say that I have made no use whatever of the Club since the New Year began, nor indeed since last summer.

I am, Sir,
Your obd. Servt.
W. E. Gladstone.

The committee discussed this letter at its meeting on April 3rd, and the secretary was instructed to write to Gladstone again.

Sir,

I am directed by the Committee of the Carlton Club in acknowledging the receipt of your letter of the 29th ultimo to observe that the subscription to the Club is *due* on the 1st day of January each year, and that non-payment on the 1st of May terminates the Membership.

At the same time the Committee feel it due to Mr. Gladstone to state that such termination is arrived at by the way of default, leaving it to his option to take such course as he may deem preferable.

I remain, Sir,
Your obedient hble. Servant
Wm. Rainger
Secretary

The minutes are silent as to the course which Gladstone finally adopted, but this marked the end of his twenty-seven years' membership of the Club. Incidentally, there would not appear to have been so great a stigma as in later years attaching to expulsion from a club for non-payment of subscription, for both Isaac Butt[1], who had originally been elected in 1852, and Lord Stratford de Redcliffe had their membership of the Carlton terminated in this way. In addition to Gladstone another prominent Peelite, the Duke of Newcastle, withdrew from the Club, though a little earlier, that is to say in 1855.

Possibly because of the example set by Gladstone and Newcastle in drifting away from the Conservative Party, the committee in the 'fifties seem to have been particularly solicitous as to the Club's fair name. On January 17th, 1854, for example, Lord Colville[2] brought to its notice a letter which had appeared in *The Times* on the previous day from Greville, the diarist and at that time clerk to the council, and upon which the *Globe* had based a leading article. After some discussion it was decided to send Greville the following letter:

> Carlton Club
> Pall Mall
> Jany 17/1854

Sir,

In a letter published by you in the *Times* of Monday last, you are pleased to assert that "some Member of the Carlton Club has put forth a laboured argument to prove that His Royal Highness Prince Albert is legally incapable of being a Privy Councillor etc., etc.

I am directed by the Committee of Management to ask upon what authority you make that assertion.

> I have the honour to be, Sir,
> your most obed[t] Servant
> Wm. Rainger,

C. C. Greville, Esqr.　　　　　　　　　　　　Secty.
Bruton Street

[1] Born 1813, died 1879. M.P. successively for Harwich, Youghal, and Limerick. Creator of the phrase "Home Rule", and first leader of the Irish Nationalist Party.
[2] The 10th Lord. Born 1818, died 1903. A Scottish Peer. Chairman of the Great Northern Railway, 1880–95. Chamberlain to the Princess of Wales 1873-1901, and to the Queen Consort 1901–03. Created a U.K. Baron 1885, and U.K. Viscount 1902.

The committee took the matter so seriously that they adjourned until the following day when in addition to Lord Colville there were also present Lord Colchester, Lord Claud Hamilton, M.P., and Mr. R. C. Heldyard, M.P. Greville had replied promptly, and his somewhat curt letter was laid before them:

> Bruton Street
> Jany. 18/1854

Sir,

I received your letter late last night; an enquiry similar to yours had been made in a letter addressed to me by "A Member of the Carlton" in the *Morning Herald*, to which I wrote an answer, which appears in the *Herald* this morning, & to which letter I beg to refer you.

> I am, Sir,
> your obt. Servt.
> C. C. Greville.

It may be doubted whether the committee relished being treated in this off-hand manner, but there was nothing they could do about it, so a further letter was sent to Greville:

> Carlton Club
> Pall Mall
> Jany. 18th, 1854

Sir,

I am directed by the Managing Committee of the Carlton Club to acknowledge the receipt of your note of the 18th inst., referring them to a letter published by you this day in the *Morning Herald* wherein you assert that you were not aware that there was a Conservative Club distinct from the Carlton, and apologize to the Carlton for the mistake into which you were thereby led.

Inasmuch as the mistake for which you acknowledge that you owe an apology appeared originally in the *Times*, the Committee

have directed me to transmit copies of this correspondence to
that paper for insertion.

> I remain, Sir,
> your obd^t. Servt.
> Wm. Rainger
> Secty.

With this the incident apparently closed.

In general, the committee were clearly trying to avoid
pushing matters to extremes where differences within the
party were concerned, as had always been their policy, but
there were occasions when some, at least, of the members
would have preferred them to take more vigorous action: in
April 1855, for example, the following letter was laid before
them:

Gentlemen,

I beg respectfully to call your attention to the speech of Lord
Monck[1] on the hustings at Portsmouth in alluding to a charge
made against him by the electors (and also by his opponent Mr.
Justice Gazelle) of being a Member of the Carlton Club to which
he replied, "he was so" but of the most liberal party "of politics",
and was admitted before he entered Parliament.

I beg also to add that I have ascertained that Lord Monck is a
Member of Brooks's Club. Under these circumstances it does
appear to be absolutely necessary some steps should be at once
adopted by the Committee and the Members of the Carlton Club
to get rid of and exclude from our society all persons avowing
such principles as Lord Monck has done, and particularly that any
person being a Member of Brooks's Club should be disqualified
for being a Member of the Carlton Club.

> I remain
> Gentlemen
> yours obediently
> Geo. Macartney.

[1]The 4th Lord. Born 1819, died 1894. An Irish Peer. M.P. for Portsmouth
1852–57. Governor-General of British America, 1867–68. Given a U.K. peerage
1866. Became a Liberal Unionist in 1886.

According to the minutes there was "a very long discussion" on this letter, and at the end of it a resolution was passed to the effect that "the Committee are of opinion that it is not at present expedient to take any steps in reference to Lord Monck's speech at Portsmouth", and Macartney was to be so informed. That was in April, but in the following August Monck resigned from the Club, so Macartney's protest may have served its purpose: furthermore, as mentioned in the previous chapter, two years later the committee laid down the rule that in future candidates must not hold political views at variance with those of the bulk of the members.

Before the summer was out, however, the good name of the Club had again been publicly impugned, and this time the matter was brought to the notice of the committee by the Chief Whip, Sir William Jolliffe, as a result of the receipt of this letter:

Sir,
I doubt not the attention of the Committee of the Carlton Club has been called to the report in the newspapers of the trial Grant v. Guinness in which Mr. Carnsew is made to appear as the agent of the Carlton Club.

I have only recently discovered that there is no foundation for this statement having been led from his representations that he was the agent of the Club, and the accredited agent of the Conservative Party and in constant communication with Sir W. Jolliffe, which induced me to place myself in his hands, the result of which has been the loss of a large sum of money, and the position in which I now am as the unseated member for Barnstaple; as I am not the only party who has thus been imposed upon I trust the Committee will take some steps to disabuse the public mind on the subject.

I am, Sir
your obed. Servant
John Laurie.

Doubtless under the stimulus of Jolliffe the committee acted as promptly as they had done in respect of Greville's allegations, and a letter was drafted for publication in *The Times*, the *Daily News*, and the *Morning Herald*.

Grant v. Guinness, M.P.

Sir,

In your report of the first portion of the above trial on the 30th ultimo, a Mr. Carnsew is described as the agent of this Club, and during the subsequent progress of the trial the accuracy of this statement seems to have been assumed.

I am directed by the Committee, who have had their attention called to this statement, to request you to do them the favour of publishing their unqualified contradiction of it, Mr. Carnsew never having been connected with the Carlton Club in any capacity whatever or authorized by it to use its name.

I am, Sir,
Your obed. Sert.
Wm. Rainger,
Secretary.

Jolliffe was not one of those Conservative Chief Whips who disinterested himself from the affairs of the Club, for he played a prominent part in its running. His eldest son, who was in the Guards, died of cholera before Sebastopol in the previous year, and his second, to quote a letter from Disraeli to Mrs. Brydges Willyams, "and prime hope, charged with Lord Cardigan at Balaclava, and after a fortnight's terrible existence under the telegraphic bulletin, that reported the whole of the light cavalry as destroyed, turned up as one of the three officers in his regiment of Dragoons who was unscathed; but the father looks ten years older than he did last session". In view of the close connection which Jolliffe maintained between the Whips' Office and the Carlton it was only fitting that on February 26th, 1861, it was decided to post the following notice in the Club:

There being a general feeling throughout the Conservative Party that the services rendered to it by Sir William Jolliffe demand public recognition on his retirement from the post that he has held for so long a period to the great benefit of that Party,

It is proposed to present his portrait painted by Grant to Lady Jolliffe, in testimony of the regard and esteem entertained towards him.

The subscription to be limited to one guinea.

Committee

The Marquess of Salisbury
The Earl of Derby
The Earl of Dalkeith, M.P.
Viscount Ingestre, M.P.
Lord Stanley, M.P.
Lord Colville
The Right Hon. B. Disraeli, M.P.
The Right Hon. J. W. Henley, M.P.

In 1866 Sir William Jolliffe was raised to the peerage as Lord Hylton.

It may have been due to his influence that the following entry is to be found in the minutes:

16.II.1864.

That the Committee having considered the prospectus of a new political club, to be called the Junior Carlton, do most cordially approve of the project, and will give it every assistance in its power.

This attitude was very different from that adopted when the Conservative Club had been founded, and it inaugurated a period of unbroken friendly relations between the Carlton and the Junior Carlton which has continued down to the present day.

When we come to the 'seventies it is to find that a different policy was apparently being pursued with regard to the appropriation of the Club's funds for political purposes.

22.III.1870.

Proposed by Lord Colville.
Seconded by Col. Rt. Hon. E. Taylor.

That in accordance with the resolution carried at the Annual Meeting of the Club on the 8th May, 1869 – The sum of £500 be advanced on account, out of the estimated surplus of £1,600, for appropriation to party purposes.

Agreed.

On February 14th of the following year an identical resolution was passed except that the sum appropriated was £900. What was the nature of the resolution passed at the annual meeting in 1869 it is impossible to say as the minute books of the annual meetings have not survived, but it would appear that the decision was to devote a certain percentage of the Club's profits to party purposes. It is true that there is no further reference to the matter in the minutes of the committee of management after 1871, but that argues nothing, for at this period these minutes were very badly kept and most uninformative.

One great political celebration did mark the Club's life during these years, and its origin is thus recorded:

16.VII.1878.

It was resolved unanimously that Lord Beaconsfield be invited to a Banquet by the Members of the Carlton Club, and that the following be a deputation to invite the Prime Minister,

The Earl of Redesdale
The Lord Hunniker
The Right Honble. Sir Jas. Fergusson, Bart.
Col. the Right Honble. E. Taylor, M.P.

"Peace with Honour", however, was not to go wholly unchallenged even in the Carlton Club, for at the end of the following year Lord Derby, who had broken with the Prime Minister over his foreign policy, took his name off the books.

CHAPTER III

Running a Victorian Club

W HAT has become known as the Victorian Era was as slow in arriving as it was in departing, and this characteristic is clearly reflected in the habits and customs of the earlier members of the Carlton Club. During the first years of the Queen's reign the atmosphere was that of the days of her uncles, and it is not until the late 'forties that one finds conditions beginning to approximate to what they were in the youth of many members still alive. Similarly, it was not until the outbreak of the First World War that Victorianism can really be said to have come to an end, as we shall see in due course.

So far as the management of the Club was concerned the committee was as vigilant as ever, and not even the most trifling matters could, apparently, be decided until they had been brought before it, so, on August 20th, 1839, after mature deliberation it was ordered that "the holes in the Water Closet seats throughout the House to be cut larger". The committee still met once a week, but in the late 'forties one can begin to detect changes in the social habits of those who composed it. Saturday afternoon meetings were abandoned in favour of Tuesday, and during August and September the attendances were liable to be very thin; sometimes, indeed, there was no one present at all. Also, people were beginning to dine later, and on October 14th, 1851, it was ordered "that the time for serving the joints in the coffee-room be advanced 15 minutes each joint, viz., to 6¼, ¼ to 7, & 7¼ o'clock". It is not, however, until July 8th, 1856, that there is any mention of lunch in the minutes, but on that date the following entry occurs: "The sub-committee suggested that a time should be fixed at which luncheons should be considered to terminate. Resolved that 4 o'clock be the hour fixed for luncheons to cease." This ruling was at once disputed, and a week later it was modified: "Complaints read from the Marquess of Salisbury and Lord Dynevor[1] respecting the alteration of the hour at which luncheon should cease; resolved, that the hour be altered from 4 P.M. to 5 P.M."

In 1846 the first change of secretary took place, for on July 14th of that year the committee passed the following somewhat ambiguous resolution: "Resolved that the Committee of Management, having decided to make great alterations in the duties of the Secretary of the Club for which the past habits of Mr. Jephson would hardly qualify him, find themselves under the necessity of stating this opinion. The Committee at the same time desire unanimously to express their sense of the zeal and fidelity with which Mr. Jephson has discharged the duties that have heretofore attached to the situation he has so long filled." What these "past habits" were is nowhere specified, but they cannot have been of a reprehensible nature for Jephson was given eighteen months' salary. He was succeeded by the steward, William Rainger, at a salary of £400 a year "not to board in the House", and the new secretary had "to give two securities in the penal sum of £2,000, to be drawn up in the same terms as Bond given by him on being nominated Steward in February, 1835".

[1] The 4th Lord. Born 1795, died 1869. M.P. for Carmarthen 1820-31 and 1832-52.

During the earlier years of Rainger's secretaryship there occurred an incident of an extremely unpleasant nature, though it was not to be wholly unparalleled in the later history of the Club. It related to the behaviour of one Sir John Cave, Bt., and the full flavour of the episode can best be appreciated from the extracts from the minutes which described it as it was from time to time reported to the committee.

4.XI.1851.

The attention of the Committee having been drawn to the injury done to an arm-chair in the morning-room by Sir John Cave, resolved that the Secretary be directed to inform him that the expense of repairing it must be charged to him.

Various Members having suggested to the Committee the great inconvenience caused to the Club in general by Sir John Cave entering the Club in his present state of health, Resolved that the Secretary be requested to intimate to Sir John Cave that it is the opinion of the Committee that his withdrawal from the Club while his present indisposition continues would be most desirable.

It is nowhere stated what was actually wrong with Sir John, but the presumption would seem to be that he was suffering from *delirium tremens*, or something not far short of it.

16.XII.1851.

The Committee of Management directed on the 4th of November a communication to be made to Sir John B. Cave, Bt., on the subject of an intolerable nuisance that had been complained of, and at the same time, in reference to the state in which Sir John Cave was in the habit, under the present unhappy condition of his health, of presenting himself at the Club, suggested the expediency of his ceasing to frequent the Club during its continuance; no attention having been paid to their suggestions, and as repeated complaints of annoyance continue to be brought before the Committee, they feel compelled to announce to Sir J. B. Cave that if he shall persevere in frequenting the Carlton Club, until his health shall be sufficiently improved to admit of his doing so without annoyance to the Members generally, it will be their painful duty, either to call a General Meeting of the Club on the subject, or to adopt such measures as fall within their own power to vindicate their authority, and to remedy the annoyances complained of.

The committee seem to have been as tolerant of the social eccentricities as of the political vagaries of the members, for in spite of this strongly-worded resolution there is no further reference to Sir John for another eight months.

31.VIII.1852.
It having been represented that Sir John Cave, Bt., notwithstanding the unhappy state in which he now is, which involves the necessity of his being attended by one of Dr. Sutherland's keepers, is in the habit of frequenting the Club, and remaining in it for hours while the keeper remains in the Hall, it is decided that the Porter do not permit the keeper to have access to and remain in the Hall.

Six more months elapsed, and then matters came to a head. On March 1st, 1853, two items engaged the attention of the committee at its meeting that day. First of all the Duke of Buckingham called attention to "the unfair way in which Members helped themselves to the rice pudding". This problem was duly considered in all its aspects, and then "the Steward was desired by the Committee to point out upon all future occasions to any Members who may help themelves unfairly, the impropriety of so doing".

The Duke then turned to the behaviour of Sir John Cave when he made the following statement:

That at 1 o'clock of the morning of Sunday last, the 27th ulto., as he was quitting the Club House, he found a mob collected about the door, and Sir John Cave supported against the railings by the Landlord of the Star and Garter Public House, from whence, assisted by his barman, he had brought him in a state of beastly drunkeness.

The minutes continue:

Several Members of the Committee having also testified to the frequent appearance of Sir John in that state, even before noon, to the great annoyance of Members and discredit of the Club, it was unanimously resolved,

That Sir John Cave be written to requesting that he will withdraw from the Club in consequence of his conduct being such as to outrage the Rules of the Club, which (Rule 28) enjoin it as a duty of the Committee to submit to a General Meeting of the Club the conduct of any individual endangering its welfare and good order, and informing him unless his name shall have been withdrawn previous to the 17th inst., it will be submitted to the General Meeting to be held on that day with a view to his removal from the List of Members.

A week later the matter came up again:

The Secretary reported that he had enclosed a copy of the resolution, passed at the last meeting, to Sir John Cave, and that he had placed the same in the hands of the Hall Porter for delivery. The latter was called in and stated that he delivered the letter to Sir John Cave on the morning of Wednesday, the 2nd inst., at which time he was far from sober.

He also informed the Committee that Sir John is in the habit of calling almost daily for his letters about 11 o'clock, and that he is invariably in the same state. Sir John has not, however, upon any occasion since the delivery to him of the resolution of the 1st inst. proceeded further than the entrance hall.

Another week passed, and then a letter was read from Sir John Cave resigning from the Club.

He was not, however, the only member to give trouble to the committee, for there was also his fellow baronet, Sir William Fraser, who seems to have been a minor nuisance over a period of years in the middle of the century: he was irascible and unreasonable rather than eccentric or alcoholic.

6.III.1855.

Complaint read from Sir William Fraser, Bt. The Secretary was instructed to write to Sir William and at the same time to inform him that a representation had been made to the Committee that Sir William Fraser's servant had ordered breakfast to be placed upon the table at 11 o'clock precisely, and that Sir William did not enter the Club until one hour afterwards, at which time he ordered a second breakfast. The Steward had charged one shilling extra, which being objected to, the Committee desired that Sir William be informed they considered the charge to be correct, and to request it may be paid to the Steward.

The effect of this communication may have been to secure an improvement in Sir William's behaviour, but if so it was of a temporary nature, for six years later the sub-committee which dealt with members' complaints brought to the notice of the committee of management not only the frequent complaints which he made, but also the terms in which he made them. The committee called in the steward and the head waiter, who both bore witness to the fact that Fraser had on more than one occasion defaced the bills of fare in the coffee-room: he was thereupon written to again:

Carlton Club
Feby. 5th, 1861.

Sir,

Your complaints respecting your dinners and other matters have been laid by the sub-committee before the Committee of Management.

I am directed by them to acquaint you that they have given

directions that the Rules of the Committee in regard to the retaining of tables in the dining-room are not to be departed from.

The Committee regret that the general arrangements of the Club should not meet with your approbation. They feel it, however, incumbent on them to remark that the terms in which your complaints are expressed render it difficult for them to give them that consideration they might otherwise desire.

I remain, Sir,

Your obd. hble. Servt

Wm. Rainger,

Secretary.

The worthy baronet seems to have been as unpopular with his fellow-members as he must have been with the committee, for not long afterwards someone struck his name out of one of the lists of members that was lying about the Club: this occasioned a further wrangle with the committee, and Sir William contrived to put himself in the wrong again.

Indeed, the committee appear to have been particularly long-suffering where he was concerned for his name crops up in the minutes repeatedly during the 'sixties and 'seventies: at first the complaints all came from him, and were concerned either with the quality of the food put before him or with the behaviour of those who waited on him. Latterly, however, it would seem that the servants launched a counter-offensive, for there were representations to the committee from them about Sir William's conduct in general and use of foul language in particular. In the spring of 1881 matters came to a head, and on May 17th of that year a sub-committee reported that "the complaint of Sir Wm. Fraser dated the 16th inst. was enquired into, and the asparagus referred to was examined, and tasted by the Committee, and found to be good". This, however, was by no means the end of the matter, for "a counter complaint made by the Steward respecting the language used by Sir William Fraser to him was then gone into, and the Committee were of opinion that the Steward must be protected, and referred the matter to the General Committee".

On the following day, accordingly, the matter was discussed there, and one cannot help feeling that there must have been a grim, and natural, determination on the part of at any rate some members of it to end the twenty-six-year-old nuisance of Sir William Fraser once and for all. Bald as is the entry in the minutes one can well imagine the feelings that lay behind it. "The Committee proceeded to consider the report of the sub-committee in reference to the complaint made by the Steward against Sir Wm. Fraser for having used threatening language to him on the night of the 16th inst. The following witnesses were examined,

> "Viscount Ranelagh
> Thomas Price, Esq.
> The Steward
> Extra Waiter Ballantine
> Waiter Cox

and the Committee decided upon addressing a letter to Sir Wm. Fraser informing him that such a complaint had been made, and asking him for an explanation either in writing before Tuesday next, the 24th inst., or by personal attendance at 2.30 P.M. on that day when the Committee will meet to consider the matter."

Those conversant with clubs and their ways will not be surprised to learn that there was a very large attendance at the meeting on May 24th. A duke and a marquess were present, while the lesser members of the peerage, baronets, and privy councillors were so numerous that there must have been a good deal of jockeying for position, or at any rate to find a seat. However, bullying servants is one thing while appearing before a club committee is quite another matter, and Sir William did not make a personal appearance – probably to the disappointment of the committee – but contented himself with a letter, which was duly considered, and the following reply ordered to be sent to him:

Carlton Club,
May 25th, 1881.

Sir,

I am directed by the General Committee to express their regret that you did not find it convenient to attend their meeting yesterday when the statements of the Steward and others, together with your letter dated the 23rd inst., were considered.

The Committee were of opinion that having regard to the numerous complaints extending over a series of years which have been brought before them relative to your conduct, and the annoyance to which Members of the Club have for so long a time been subjected, they would fail in their duty if they did not bring the whole matter before a General Meeting, and they have accordingly decided to call one for that purpose, of which due notice will be given under Rule 29.

I am further to inform you that previous complaints against you will be brought under the notice of the General Meeting, and I enclose to you copies of the statements made by the Steward and others, and also a copy of the notice calling a General Meeting of the Club.

I am, Sir,
Your obedient Servant
(Sigd) E. M. S. Chichester,
Secy.

Sir William Fraser, Bt.

There the matter would appear to have rested until June 7th, when a letter was received from Lord Ormathwaite, enclosing one from Sir William Fraser, but we have no clue to the contents of either. The general meeting was held on the 13th, and the committee met immediately afterwards, when it "settled the form of the Minutes of the General Meeting, and ordered that a copy of the resolution passed by the meeting should be sent to Sir Wm. Fraser". What happened at the general meeting we do not know, but Sir William remained a member until his death at the end of the century, and to judge by the complaints which he continued to make neither his temper nor his manner improved with the passing years. He was not so colourful a personality as Sir John Cave, but he must have been a very unpleasant fellow to have in a club.

Direct action in the coffee-room, which, as we have seen, was one of Sir William Fraser's earlier excesses was not, however, peculiar to him, for during this period there was a far more illustrious offender, namely that pillar of the Club and of Conservatism, the second Marquess of Salisbury; for on April 4th, 1848, the committee was informed that on two successive days during the previous week he had "wilfully broken down" the dinner boards in the coffee-room. His colleagues thereupon ordered that the boards should be immediately repaired and that the expense of so doing should be defrayed by Lord Salisbury, and a rider was added to the effect that "The Committee in communicating this resolution desires to express their regret that the circumstances should have occurred". At the next meeting the following letter was read: "The Marquess of Salisbury presents his compts. to the Committee of the Carlton Club, and in answer to their letter fully admits his liability to pay for the damage done by him to the furniture of the dining-room." There the matter ended, but it was not until another two months had passed that Lord Salisbury again attended a meeting of the committee.

This was an exceptional case, but from time to time difficulty was experienced in persuading the members to comply with the ordinary rules. On December 18th, 1855, for example, the steward "reported that T. I. Langford Brooke, Esqr., had ordered two glasses of brandy and water to be served in the Front Hall for himself and a cab man, and that he continued to smoke in the Front Hall after being told it was contrary to the regulations of the Committee". The offender was brought to book with the following letter:

> Carlton Club,
> December 18/1855.
>
> Sir,
> I am directed by the Committee of Management to state that they have been informed that on the evening of Thursday, December the 6th, you violated the regulation of the Club by insisting on having two glasses of brandy and water supplied to you in the Front Hall, and also by smoking there.
>
> The Committee desire me to express their hope that such an irregularity may not again occurr, especially as had the Club Servants obeyed your orders they would have been liable to be dismissed.
>
> I am, Sir,
> Your obedient Servant
> Wm. Rainger,
> Secretary.

The committee of those days had very definitely set its face against what seems to have become the growing custom of smoking in the Front Hall, and five years earlier they had put it on record that they felt "it to be their duty to state that in the event of any Members being again reported to them as having smoked in the Front Hall, a General Meeting of the Club will be called, at which the statement of the fact, and the name or names of the few Members thus disregarding regulations passed for the general convenience, will be laid before the Club". In these circumstances Mr. Langford Brooke was lucky to get off with a letter of admonition; but perhaps he knew that the committee's bark was worse than its bite.

The servants seem to have been quite ready to co-operate with the committee in enforcing the rules, for on December 27th, 1853, we find the night porter informing it that "Mr. Hume took a gentleman, not a Member of the Club, this evening into the library for nearly an hour contrary to the rules of the Club; when I informed Mr. Hume that it was against the rules he said that he had a right to show a gentleman over the House, and used language quite uncalled for while respectfully performing my duty". Perhaps if Mr. Hume had been more restrained in his language the committee would never have heard of his breach of the rules.

However this may be, the secretary was instructed to reprove him in the following terms:

Sir,

The Night Porter having represented to the Committee that on Thursday last, the 22nd inst., after the hour of 10 o'clock at night you introduced a Gentleman into the library, he not being a Member of the Club; that he was there for a considerable time, and that upon the Porter respectfully representing to you, in accordance to his duty, that this was contrary to the Rules of the Club, you appeared to have taken offence at his so doing; the Committee beg me to inform you that it is a perfectly well recognized rule of this and other Clubs that no use whatever can be permitted to be made of the Club by any stranger, and that though it has been the custom to allow Members to show a friend over the House during the day time, it would be extremely inconvenient if such a privilege was acted upon at a late hour of the evening.

I am, Sir,

your most obd. Servt.

Wm. Rainger,

Secretary.

Mr. Hume, who was the grandfather of the first Viscount Long of Wraxall, later changed his name to Dick, and was M.P. for Wicklow from 1852 to 1880. If this incident be a reliable guide to his normal behaviour, he was more voluble in Pall Mall than at Westminster, for he only addressed the House of Commons once, and that was when he spoke for three minutes in support of a Bill to prohibit pigeon-shooting.

Although visitors were not admitted into the Club they were allowed to wait for members in the hall, a custom which would not have been tolerated in a later day. The only regular exception was, as we have seen, in the case of ladies on the rare occasions when a procession passed along Pall Mall. However, on April 16th, 1872, the committee agreed that "23 Members of Parliament for Cheshire and Lancashire, three of whom are not Members of the Club, be allowed the use of the House dining room for their annual dinner. This permission not to be regarded as a precedent for the admission of strangers to dine at the Club". All the same a precedent had been created, and it was soon to be utilized in the case of a very distinguished visitor indeed, for on November 28th, 1876, the committee was informed that "H.R.H. the Prince of Wales had intimated that he was desirous of dining at a House dinner at the Carlton Club", to which the reply was that "The Club will feel honoured by his presence." On February 11th of the following year the Prince duly dined at the Club.

Its place in the social and political life of London at this time is well illustrated by the frequent contemporary references to it. When, for instance, Disraeli, then Leader of the Opposition, returned from the thanksgiving service at St. Paul's on February 27th, 1872, for the recovery of the Prince of Wales, it was to the Carlton that he naturally went to discuss the events of the day:

On returning from St. Paul's, Disraeli met with an overpowering "ovation"; I should say "triumph", for he was in his chariot. This not only continued from the City to Waterloo Place; but his carriage, ascending Regent Street, turning to the right[1] along Oxford Street, and thence back to the Carlton Club, the cheers which greeted him from all classes convinced him that, for the day at least, a more popular man did not exist in England.

Soon after his return I happened to pass into the morning-room of the Carlton Club. Disraeli was leaning against the table immediately opposite to the glass door, wearing the curious white coat which he had for years occasionally put on over his usual dress. Familiar as I was with his looks and expression, I never saw him with such a countenance as he had at that moment. I have heard it said by one who spoke to Napoleon I at Orange in France, that his face was as that of one who looks into another world: that is the only description I can give of Disraeli's look at the moment I speak of. He seemed more like a statue than a human being: never before nor since have I seen anything approaching it: he was ostensibly listening to Mr. Sclater Booth, now Lord Basing. In the afternoon I said to the latter, "What was Disraeli talking about when I came into the room?" He replied, "About some county business; I wanted his opinion." I said, "I will tell you what he was thinking about: he was thinking that he will be Prime Minister again." I had no doubt at the time; nor have I ever doubted since.[2]

[1] "Right" is presumably a mistake for "left". The carriage was probably going to drop Lady Beaconsfield at Grosvenor Gate before taking her husband to the Carlton.
[2] Fraser, Sir William: *Disraeli and His Day*, pp. 374–6.

To pass from the behaviour of the members to that of the servants is to find a much happier state of affairs than that which prevailed in the earlier years of the Club's history, though it is, of course, possible that as there was now a special sub-committee to deal with them their delinquencies were not brought to the notice of the Committee of Management as had been the case in the past. On July 1st, 1857, a general increase of wages was granted, and it is not uninteresting to see the rates which then prevailed:

The Steward from	£160	to	£180
Groom of the Chambers	50	,,	60
Hall Porter	42	,,	45
Under Butler	35	,,	40
Coffee-room waiters	26	,,	30
Waiter out of livery	26	,,	30
Drawing-room waiter	26	,,	30
Night Porter	26	,,	28
House Porter	26	,,	28

Females

Housekeeper	£52	,,	£55
1st Still Room Maid	25	,,	26
2nd ,, ,, Maid	15	,,	18
1st Housemaid	20	,,	21
2nd ,,	14	,,	16
3rd ,,	13	,,	14
4th ,,	12	,,	13
5th ,,	11	,,	12
6th ,,	11	,,	12

These wages were paid quarterly until 1877, when the secretary reported to the committee that the servants would prefer to receive their money monthly, and this was accordingly arranged. The servants enumerated above did not represent the whole staff, for in March 1842 there are references to a messenger who was paid £21 a year, "but as he performs his duties promptly and well, the Sub-Committee thinks his wages may be increased to £25, his book realizing about that sum". On the same date the billiard boy and the hall boy are shown as receiving £8 and £10 respectively, and it was suggested that they should each receive a rise of £2. How many of these servants lived in it is impossible to say, but the "Committee decided to allow £5 to each servant finding accommodation out of the House".

The servants' hours were certainly long, as is shown by an entry in the minutes under date of March 28th, 1854:

In consequence of the number of hours the servants are obliged to be on duty, viz., from 7 o'clock A.M. until 3 or 4 o'clock the next morning, being upwards of 20 hours, the Committee direct that the following notice shall be placed in the smoking-room.

The Committee beg to call the attention of Members to the inconvenience sustained by the general service of the Club from the House being frequently kept open to various hours from 2 till 5 in the morning, by a very few Gentlemen remaining in it after all the other Members have retired.

According to the strict Rule of the Club the House is closed at 2 o'clock, or if the Houses of Parliament sit to a later hour, at one hour after they have risen.

Resolved that for the present the order of opening the House at 8 o'clock A.M. be suspended, and the Club be opened at 9 o'clock A.M. as heretofore.

One incident there was at the beginning of the period under review which must have been the subject of much comment among the members:

27.VIII.1844.
A letter from Cattermole, late Night Porter, was read in which he requested a reconsideration of his discharge ordered on the 13th inst. It having been stated by both the Secretary and the Steward that Cattermole had expressed to them a desire that the Committee should be made aware that he could, if discharged

make certain disclosures which would be discreditable and detri-
mental to the character of the Club, he was called in and at once
admitted the fact, and avowed that he had obtained through
listening at the doors of the drawing- and smoking-rooms a
knowledge of which he thought he had a right to take advantage,
and which would be an awkward bill of fare to bring before the
public.

The committee refused to be blackmailed, and resolved
"that Cattermole should be discharged forthwith".

In the early 'sixties there would appear to have been a
crisis of some sort in the internal affairs of the Club but it is
not easy to determine its exact nature: perhaps its origin is to
be found in the wild rumours which from time to time get
round in a club regarding its management or the reliability
of some official. At any rate on April 23rd, 1861, the Marquess
of Salisbury, the Hon. Stuart Knox, and Captain John
Hamilton were appointed as a sub-committee to enquire into
the subject of the regular payment of the bills, and they reported in due course that they had discovered "no defalcations in
the accounts of the Club", but that "Mr. Rainger committed
great irregularity in holding over at various times monies
received by him." The secretary was duly advised of this
finding, but no further action was taken so far as he personally
was concerned. He had, it may be mentioned, been agitating
for an increase in his salary during the previous five years,
though without success: all he got, in March 1856 was a
gratuity of £100 for his services during the move into the
new premises; he was clearly none too pleased with this,
and in his letter of thanks he expressed the hope that a permanent rise would not be long delayed. The committee did
not take the hint.

On the contrary, after receiving the report of the sub-committee in the spring of 1861 a thorough reorganization of the Club's financial management was put in hand, the accounting system was changed, and a quarterly audit by a firm of professional accountants was introduced. One gets the impression that Rainger, though apparently personally honest, was too set in his ways to approve of these innovations. However this may be, at a meeting of the committee on March 4th, 1862, he resigned, and he was not asked to reconsider his decision. In the following June he was given a pension of £100 a year, and a Colonel Sutton was chosen in his place. The new secretary had one very serious demerit from the point of view of posterity, in that in his regime the minutes became jejune in the extreme, and are very little guide to what members were thinking or doing.

Fourteen years later there was another crisis, apparently of a similar nature. Nothing in Colonel Sutton's very abbreviated minutes gives any clue to the trouble which must have been brewing, until on March 21st, 1876, there appears the unheralded entry, "A letter was read from the Secretary placing his resignation in the hands of the Committee." Consideration was deferred until the following week, when a resolution was passed that "the Committee having full confidence in Colonel Sutton, and in view of the discussion which must take place at the next General Meeting, decline to accept his resignation". During the next few weeks there are several uninformative references to this general meeting which had been summoned on the requisition of the stipulated number of members, and on May 9th the committee decided to put to that meeting the suggestion that six members, three to be selected by the committee and three at the general meeting, should form a special body "to report on the management of the Club".

The general meeting was held on May 13th, with Lord Redesdale in the chair, and the appointment of this special committee seems to have been agreed to: no report of the proceedings has survived though a remuneration of £20 was voted to the shorthand writer who took them down, which seems a considerable sum of money for those days. All through June and July a series of meetings of one sort and another took place, and it is difficult to resist the conclusion that the gathering storm-clouds in the Near East probably escaped the notice of many members in consequence. At an extraordinary general meeting on July 4th it was agreed that "the internal management of the Club, subject to the approval of the General Committee, shall be entrusted to a Sub-Committee, to be called the House Committee, consisting of nine Members, three of whom shall retire annually in rotation, and the vacancies so caused shall be filled by the three Members of the Committee, elected on the nomination of individual Members of the Club".

It is difficult, for want of evidence, to discover exactly what was at issue, but this resolution seems to have satisfied everybody except the secretary who, like Rainger before him, thought the old ways were best. However this may be, on July 11th he again handed in his resignation, but a resolution was unanimously carried to the effect that "as Colonel Sutton has the confidence of the Committee, and has been thoroughly exonerated from all blame by the Select Committee appointed at the Second Annual General Meeting of the Club on the 13th May last, he be requested to withdraw his resignation". Nevertheless Colonel Sutton had had enough, and he refused to change his mind. A pension of £300 a year was granted to him, which was much more generous treatment than that accorded to his predecessors, and at the beginning

of 1877 his place was taken by E. Manners Sutton Chichester.
Thereafter the minutes again become more informative.

In retrospect, as no doubt also to contemporary members,
the prices charged for meals are of particular interest. The
first occasion on which the minutes contain anything like a
full tariff was July 25th, 1876, when a resolution was passed
to the effect that "the custom of charging even sixpences in
the Club be abolished, and the following prices be charged
for the various articles supplied to Members, such prices to be
revised from time to time by the Committee according to
the cost of the articles". A list of prices followed:

Soups			6d. to 1s.
Hot Joints,	including Potatoes		1s. 6d.
Second help	,,	,,	1s.
Large Steak	,,	,,	1s. 6d.
Small ,,	,,	,,	1s.
Mutton Chop	,,	,,	9d.
Second ,,	,,	,,	6d.
Cold Meats	,,	,,	1s.
Second help	,,	,,	6d.
Ham	,,	,,	1s.
Tongue	,,	,,	1s.
Sandwiches, Ham or Beef			6d.
,, Chicken			1s.
Meat Pies, portion			1s.
Chicken Pies, portion			1s. 6d.
Galantine Pies, portion			1s. 6d.
2 Poached Eggs			6d.
Mayonnaise, Salmon			1s.
,, Chicken			2s. 6d.
,, ,, half-portion			1s. 3d.
Salad			6d.
Lemon 1d. Pat of Butter 1d.			
Bread and Cheese, and Pat of Butter			6d.

Beer per glass 1d., tankard 2d.
Soda Water, Ginger Beer, etc.   3d.
Seltzer and Lithia   4d.
Apollinaris   5d.

Five years later the House Committee was instructed to examine the tariff again, and it reported in favour of the abolition of table money at lunch: it also suggested a new list of charges, which duly came into force on June 1st, 1881.

Soups		6d. to 1s. as at present	
Hot Joints	{ Beef	1s.	
	Mutton	1s.	
	Poultry	2s.	
Cold	{ Mutton		
	Ham	6d. to 1s.	
	Tongue	as at present	
	Pies		
	Galantine		
Mutton Chop		6d.	
Steaks		1s. to 1s. 6d.	
Lemons		1d. each	
Pat of Butter		1d.	
Cheese, ordinary		2d.	
Foreign Cheeses		6d.	
Stilton and Cream			
Potatoes (old)		2d.	
„ mashed or fried		4d.	
Cabbage		2d.	
Beer		1d. per tumbler	
		2d. per goblet	
Currant Jelly		2d.	
Poached Eggs as at present			
Mayonnaise of Fish, according to price of fish			
Beetroot		3d.	
Salads – Potatoes		3d.	

| Lettuce { | June
July
August | 3d. |

| „ | other months | 6d. |
| Cream | | 3d. |

From these tariffs it would not appear that there had been any marked change in the price of food during the five years which separated them.

Other comparable, and not uninteresting, figures to be found in the minutes at this period relate to the rateable value of the Club. On July 19th, 1853, it was reported to the committee that a new assessment had been made by the Parish authorities, and "the Rateing of the Club has been increased from £2,340 to £2,700, being £360 per annum". The committee were clearly annoyed at this increase, but they decided to agree to it "rather than incur the cost of litigation". There is a further reference to the matter on September 17th, 1878, where the rateable value of the Pall Mall clubs is given as follows:

	£
Army and Navy	2,834
Guards	530
Oxford and Cambridge	1,667
Junior Carlton	2,917
Carlton	3,334
Reform	2,486
Travellers	1,459
Athenaeum	1,250

These figures were produced in connection with a proposition which is illustrative of the working of local government in London at that time, for a letter "from the Treasurer of the Wood Pavement Fund" was read at this meeting of the committee "stating that they had collected the sum promised by the inhabitants of Pall Mall, viz., £425, leaving a sum of £1,775 to be contributed by the War Office and the clubs undermentioned, to complete the amount required by the Vestry, viz., £2,200. In the absence of the money promised by the War Office, the sum required is equal to a rate of 2s. 2d. in the £ upon the rateable value of the eight clubs". Whether the War Office, which then stood on the site of the present Royal Automobile Club, ever paid its share is not stated, but the figures give a good indication of the rising value of property in the West End during the mid-Victorian period.

One subject in particular made repeated appearances on the committee agenda, and that was the question of smoking. The battle between the smokers and the anti-smokers was fiercely contested and long-drawn-out, and the final victory of the smokers did not really take place until the Club was bombed in 1940, for it was only at 69 St. James's Street that smoking was permitted all over the house, except, of course, in the coffee-room. One of the earlier rounds gained by the smokers was on March 26th, 1866, when the hour at which smoking was permitted in the billiards-room was advanced from 10.0 p.m. to 8.0 p.m. Another eight years passed, and then a further advance was made, for on March 17th, 1874, it was decided that "Members be allowed to smoke and play cards in the House Dinner room after 9.0 P.M.", while by June of that year the subject had become of such importance that the Earl of Abergavenny, Lord Henry Thynne, M.P., and Lieut.-Colonel W. Honywood were appointed to serve as a "Smoking Committee". Their terms of reference are not stated, and as the minute books of the sub-committees have long since perished there is no record of their activities, but the mere fact of their appointment was a sign of the times.

On one score the committee of those days had no worries, and that was in respect of membership; indeed the number of candidates coming forward was at times clearly embarrassing. This seems to have been the case in 1877, for on May 8th of that year Sir William Hart Dyke,[1] the Chief Whip, who took as keen an interest in the affairs of the Club as Jolliffe had done, drew "the attention of the Committee to the very large and daily increasing numbers of Candidates on the books, and having mentioned that the Committee of the St. Stephen's Club were willing to admit a certain number, should they so wish, it was resolved that the St. Stephen's Club be asked to nominate three Members of their Committee to meet an equal number of Members of the Committee of this Club, to consider the proposition made to them on their behalf by Sir William Dyke, with reference to the election of Members to the former Club". The representatives of the Carlton were the Chief Whip himself, Lord Balfour of Burleigh, and the Hon. W. P. Talbot.

The outcome of this meeting between the committees of the two clubs was that the St. Stephen's agreed to accept three hundred candidates from the waiting-list of the Carlton as *interim* members for five years without the payment of any entrance fee; if at the expiration of that period any of these *interim* members wished to remain in the St. Stephen's he must then pay the entrance fee. As there are no further references to the subject presumably this scheme worked to the satisfaction of all concerned, and it well illustrates the interest which the Chief Whip still took in the fortunes of the West End Conservative clubs.

[1] The 7th Baronet. Born 1837, died 1931. On November 19th, 1867, Disraeli wrote of him to Queen Victoria: "The address to your Majesty's Speech was moved this evening by Mr. Hart Dyke, with grace and great ability: a young man, good-looking and very popular. He gained the whole House. M.P. for W. Kent."

As to the use made of the Club by the members it is not easy to arrive at even an approximate estimate: weekly returns of expenditure and receipts, and of members dining, were regularly laid before the committee, and one of these, taken at random, may be said to be typical of the summer months when, of course, the Club was most used: it is dated July 3rd, 1877:

	£	s.	d.
The Balance at the Bankers'	13,532	15	9
Expenditure	223	7	4
Receipts	160	14	5
Balance against the Club	62	12	11

	£	s.	d.
73 Servants at 12s. 6d. each	45	12	6
Loss on the Coffee-Room	17	0	5
	62	12	11

Number of Coffee-Room Dinners	385
„ „ „ Luncheons	433

At one time there seems to have been some difficulty in getting members to pay their bills, for on February 21st, 1843, it is recorded "Complaints having been made to the Committee that in several cases gentlemen have gone away without paying their bills, the Committee have ordered, with a view of giving effect to the 26th Rule of the Club, that letters should be written to them, and the Steward instructed that such persons as have received a letter from the Committee demanding payment of money due to the Club, shall not be served with anything in the coffee-room till such money shall be paid". This somewhat drastic procedure would appear to have been effective; at any rate there is no further reference to the matter, and in more recent times he would indeed have been a resolute offender who could get out of the coffee-room, let alone out of the Club, without paying what he owed.

There are one or two other items of interest in the life of the Club in these mid-Victorian days. For example, when the necessity arose the committee were clearly ready to apply their leader's maxim, *sanitas sanitatum omnia sanitas*, to the affairs of the Club, for on June 18th, 1872, they decided unanimously that "a continuous supply of water be laid on to the present urinals on the ground and entresol floors, and that the urinals be reconstructed on a better principle". Ten years earlier the modern practice was for the first time adopted of closing the Club for a month during the holiday season.

The most important innovation of all is, however, to be found in the minutes of March 1st, 1881, when the following entry occurs: "The Secretary was instructed to write again to the Telephone Co. and urge them to arrange for the wires being laid into the Club from the House of Commons, as soon as possible." With the coming of the telephone a new era in the life of the Club had clearly begun.

CHAPTER IV

The End of the Nineteenth Century

THE place of the Club in the Conservative Party, and the reactions of outside politics upon the life of the Club, down to the formation of the second Salisbury administration in 1886, have already been discussed in an earlier chapter, and attention was there called to the surprisingly little information on the subject contained in the minutes. In 1887, as will be shown in due course, a new secretary was appointed, but he was as reticent where these matters were concerned as were his predecessors. There is every reason to suppose that during these years the Political Committee was in existence and was active, but of what it did and how it did it there is no trace. There are, however, several allusions to political matters, and from these it is possible to make certain deductions, more especially when the general background is taken into consideration.

The General Election of 1886 had returned to the House of Commons 316 Conservatives, 78 Liberal Unionists, 191 Liberals, and 85 Irish Nationalists, so the Salisbury administration was dependent for its majority upon the votes of the Liberal Unionists, who had broken with Gladstone over the question of Home Rule for Ireland. As we have seen, there were occasions when it looked as if they might return to the Liberal fold, in which case Lord Salisbury and his colleagues would have found themselves in a minority; this, however,

did not happen, and with the passage of time the Liberal
Unionists approximated ever more closely to their Conservative allies. Nevertheless, they did not take office in the government; they retained their own organization both at Westminster and in the constituencies; and they were not eligible
for membership of the Carlton Club. The three years of
Opposition, which followed the return of the Liberals to
power in 1892, not unnaturally brought the Conservatives
and Liberal Unionists closer together, and in the third Salisbury administration, formed in 1895, the Liberal Unionist
leaders held office; but the separate organizations, and the in-
eligibility for election to the Carlton, remained, which accounts for the fact that men like Sir Austen Chamberlain
only became members of the Club relatively late in their
political careers.

For a brief space Lord Randolph Churchill took an active
interest in the Club's affairs, and once the question of its
position in the counsels of the Conservative Party had been
settled he was frequently present at the meetings of the committee, more particularly during the momentous year in
British politics, 1886. An even more august personage appeared at the meeting on December 12th, 1893, namely Lord
Salisbury himself, then Leader of the Opposition, and of this
event the official record says: "A proposal for the Association
of Conservative Clubs, and the appointment of delegates to
represent this Club in carrying out the same, was then discussed. Proposed by the Marquess of Salisbury, K.G., seconded by the Marquess of Carmarthen, M.P., and resolved:
That while recognizing the great desirability of bringing all
Conservative clubs into greater proximity, the Committee
resolve to adjourn the further consideration of the matter
until an early date in February, for the purpose of receiving a

fuller account of the proposed organization. The Secretary
was instructed to forward a copy of this resolution to Mr.
Middleton, the Head Agent of the Party."

Accordingly, on February 13th, 1894, the matter came up
again, when "The proposed Association of Conservative
Clubs discussed in December last was further considered. Mr.
Akers-Douglas[1] having explained the objects of the organization it was resolved that three delegates should be appointed
to represent the Club on the governing body, and the following three Members were appointed accordingly, Mr. Herbert
Praed, Marquess of Carmarthen, M.P., and Mr. H. R.
Graham, M.P.". This incident is a testimony alike to the
interest which Lord Salisbury took in the Party organization
and to the importance which he attached to the participation
of the Carlton Club.

It is also clear that the Club at this time made substantial
financial contributions for Party purposes. On July 5th, 1887,
we find the cryptic statement, "A cheque for £1,500 for
registration purposes was authorized to be drawn"; three
years later, on July 8th, 1890; the same sum was voted "for
Parliamentary expenses"; and on May 31st, 1892, "it was
decided to increase the grant for Parliamentary expenses to
£2,000 for this year only, in view of the General Election".
In 1894 the amount was £1,500, and in the following year,
when there was another general election, it was raised to
£2,000. These are the only references to the subject in the
minutes at this period, and from them it would appear to be
not unreasonable to deduce that the Club made an annual

[1] Born 1851, died 1926. Chief Whip 1883–95, First Commissioner of Works
1895–1902, Home Secretary 1902–05. Created Viscount Chilston in 1911. Mrs.
Dugdale, in her *Arthur James Balfour*, says, "Mr. Akers-Douglas, the Home
Secretary, was one of those colleagues whom all Prime Ministers cherish, steady,
wise, vastly experienced as an ex-Chief Whip; he was a stand-by throughout".

donation of £1,500 for Party purposes, which was increased to £2,000 when a general election was pending. The fact that the allocation does not appear regularly means nothing, for the minutes were not kept in any great detail. Whether the sum was paid into the Party coffers direct, or whether it was handed over the the Political Committee, we are not told, but in any case the payment was a departure from the earlier ruling that "the Committee had no funds belonging to the Club which could be appropriated to such a purpose".

In another respect, too, there was a break with tradition about this time. It will be remembered that during the internal crisis in the Conservative Party in the 'forties and 'fifties the committee had been careful to preserve a non-committal attitude in spite of the pressure on the part of some members to act otherwise, but in 1886 a very different line was taken. At the general election of the previous year the Conservative vote in the Petersfield division of Hampshire had been split, with the following result:

Viscount Wolmer L	3,414
W. Nicholson C	3,253
D. Henty C	179

On this the committee took action:

19.I.1886.

On the motion of Lord Robert Bruce, seconded by Lord Henniker, the following resolution was passed, and copies of the same were ordered to be sent to Lord Hylton[1] and Mr. Jolliffe for any remarks they may have to make thereon,

That this Committee having considered the circumstances of the Petersfield election, cannot refrain from expressing their deep

[1] The 2nd Lord. Born 1829, died 1899. He had charged with the Light Brigade at Balaclava (*vide supra*, p. 88). M.P. for Wells, 1855–68.

regret that Lord Hylton and Mr. Jolliffe should have thought it consistent with their position as Members of the Carlton Club to take so prominent and active a part in promoting the candidature of Mr. Henty against the wishes of the Local Association and the responsible authorities of the Party, to which action on the part of Lord Hylton and Mr. Jolliffe in the opinion of the Committee is directly to be attributed the loss of the seat.

Lord Hylton duly replied to this criticism of his conduct, but his letter has not been preserved. The committee, however, were not satisfied, so they passed another resolution of censure, in practically the same terms as the previous one, and ordered that it "should be placed in the Morning-Room and that Lord Hylton be so informed". This was not the end of the matter, for on February 9th a letter was brought up "from Mr. Jolliffe transmitting a memorandum signed by Lord Hylton in reference to the Petersfield election question, and after consideration the Committee instructed the Secretary to write to Mr. Jolliffe informing him that they saw no reason for reversing the decision they had arrived at".

If the committee were sticking to their guns, so was Lord Hylton, for on February 23rd, "a letter dated the 20th inst. addressed to the Committee by Lord Hylton was read, and they instructed the Secretary to inform Lord Hylton that they were unable to re-open the question, and to remind Lord Hylton that after enquiry the Resolution referred to was proposed and seconded but not discussed or adopted, and his Lordship was furnished with a copy and invited to make any explanation he desired; that his sole reply consisted of animadversions on the previous conduct of Mr. Nicholson, and the expression of his opinion that Mr. Nicholson's 'success would have been a misfortune to the Tory Party', therefore under the circumstances the Committee felt themselves justified in adopting the course they pursued". This reply strikes one as somewhat disingenuous, but possibly by this time the committee were beginning to doubt the wisdom of the action they had taken: however this may be the crisis in Petersfield itself soon subsided, for Lord Wolmer became a Liberal Unionist on the introduction of the Home Rule Bill.

This was, it may be observed, by no means the last occasion on which a member of the Club supported an independent Conservative against an official candidate, and the most famous instance of such behaviour was in February 1935, when Sir Winston Churchill and Lord Lloyd backed Mr. Randolph Churchill at a bye-election in the Wavertree division of Liverpool; as at Petersfield fifty years earlier this resulted in the loss of the seat.

Tempers seem to have been rather short in that winter of 1885–86, for at the very moment that the committee was involving itself in the Petersfield dispute it was endeavouring not to become implicated in a private political difference between Lord Bury[1] and Mr. C. E. Lewis[2], M.P. for Londonderry City; at any rate that is the impression created by the following entries in the minutes:

15.XII.1885.

A letter from Lord Bury dated the 14th inst. complaining of the conduct of Mr. C. E. Lewis was read, and the Committee instructed the Secretary to inform Lord Bury that a copy of his letter to them had been forwarded to Mr. Lewis with a request for such explanation as he could offer, and that when a reply had been received from Mr. Lewis a further communication would be addressed to Lord Bury by the Committee.

[1] Later 8th Earl of Albemarle. Born 1858, died 1942.

[2] Later Sir C. E. Lewis, Bt. He was unseated for Londonderry City on petition in 1886, and the seat was awarded to his Nationalist opponent, Justin McCarthy. He represented North Antrim, 1887–92.

22.XII.1885.

A letter addressed to the Committee by Mr. C. E. Lewis, M.P., in reply to their letter of the 14th inst. (*sic*) was considered, and it was resolved to postpone the question involved until the 13th of January next: the Committee to be specially summoned, and Lord Bury and Mr. C. E. Lewis to be so informed.

9.II.1886.

The correspondence between Lord Bury and Mr. C. E. Lewis, M.P., having been taken into consideration, the Committee desired the Secretary to write to Mr. Lewis that they declined absolutely to enter into the private differences of individual Members of the Club, that according to his own version he had commenced an altercation with Lord Bury on the 9th of December within the precincts of the Club, and amongst other expressions called him "a disgrace to the Party". The Committee therefore call upon Mr. Lewis to make a written apology to the Club, through them, and to Lord Bury, for having used that and other expressions he, Mr. Lewis, did use to him in the Club.

23.II.1886.

A letter addressed to the Committee by Mr. C. E. Lewis, M.P., dated the 16th inst., apologizing to them for his conduct within the precincts of the Club on the 9th of December last was read, and the Secretary was ordered to inform him that his apology was accepted by them as satisfactory.

A letter from Mr. C. E. Lewis, M.P., addressed to the Secretary dated this day, covering a letter from him addressed to Lord Bury apologizing to Lord Bury for the words he had used in the Dining-Room to him on the 9th of December last was read, and the Secretary was instructed to forward Mr. C. E. Lewis's letter to Lord Bury.

Thirteen years later another incident occurred which very nearly involved the committee in legal proceedings, and it well illustrates the difficult position into which those respon-

sible for running a club may be put in respect of the private
affairs of the members.

On January 31st, 1899, the secretary reported that a letter
had arrived at the Club addressed to Sir Henry Meux, and
that the Marquess of Ailesbury[1] had said that if it was given
to him he would pass it on to Sir Henry. The secretary had
refused to allow this, and the committee supported him. By
the time that the committee met again a week later a communication had been received from Messrs. Upton and Britton, solicitors, "demanding that a letter lying at this Club
addressed to Sir Henry Meux should be delivered to Lady
Meux under a power of attorney given by Sir Henry Meux
to her. Failing this they stated that proceedings would be taken
to recover it". The secretary said that he had consulted the
Club's solicitors who advised him that the committee was
not entitled to hand over the letter to anybody except Sir
Henry Meux himself. The committee agreed with this ad-
vice, and was quite prepared to fight if necessary; the Club's
solicitors were accordingly so informed.

At this point it would appear that certain private negotiations must have been going on, for when the matter next
makes its appearance in the minutes, that is to say on February 21st, both parties had receded from their original position.
A letter was then read from the Club's solicitors "stating that
Messrs. Upton and Britton had abandoned the claim for the
letter to Sir H. Meux under the power of attorney, and made
suggestions as to the disposal of the letter. The House Committee recommended that the letter should be given to Lord
Ailesbury to deliver provided that costs were paid and an
indemnity given by Messrs. Upton and Britton. This was

---

[1] The 5th Marquess. Born 1842, died 1911. He was chairman of Messrs.
Meux & Co.

agreed to". What Lord Ailesbury had to do with the matter, and why the letter could not have been given to him in the first place without all this fuss, we do not know. The final reference to this very odd affair occurs on March 3rd, when a further letter from the Club's solicitors was read to the effect that "as Lady Meux's solicitors had agreed to pay the costs of the Club, and would give the indemnity required, the letter could now be given to Lord Ailesbury. The Secretary reported that this had been done". So ended an affair which could hardly have failed to create an impression of vacillation on the part of the committee.

From time to time certain intriguing statements make their appearance in the minutes, but the subject to which they relate is tantalizingly never disclosed; for example:

24.IV.1886.

A matter affecting the character of a Member having been brought to the notice of the Committee, the Secretary was instructed to address a letter to that Member on the subject, and to request an immediate reply.

Whether the trouble was social or political there is no indication, nor is there any further reference to the matter. Perhaps when the committee received the letter from the member in question it was decided to leave well alone.

It is pleasant to note that when the Junior Constitutional Club, now, alas, a thing of the past, was founded in 1887, the committee passed a resolution that "permission be granted for circulars to be dated from the Carlton Club for the proposed Junior Constitutional Club". The subsequent connection between the two clubs can hardly be said to have been close, but individual members of the Carlton from time to time played a prominent part in the life of the Junior Constitutional.

Two of the most important events of these years were the
Golden and Diamond Jubilees of Queen Victoria, in 1887 and
1897 respectively, and both were loyally celebrated by the
Club. In the early summer of 1887 there was a Colonial Conference in London, and a general meeting of the Club empowered the committee "to invite distinguished colonial
delegates to become Honorary Members of the Club during
their visit to England". What strikes the twentieth-century
reader in connection with these celebrations is what a short
time ahead the preparations were made in comparison with
more recent practice on similar occasions. For example, the
Golden Jubilee was celebrated on June 21st, 1887, but it was
not until the 17th of the previous month that there is any
allusion to the event in the minutes, and we then read, "The
question of the arrangements for the Jubilee Day was then
considered, and it was decided that in the event of Her Majesty
passing through Pall Mall, that each Member will be permitted to introduce personally one Lady. Luncheon to be
provided at 3s. 6d. per head." Furthermore, "subject to the
Queen's passing the Club", tenders were accepted as follows:

For erecting a staging over the area, covering with red cloth, and enclosing the entrance, etc.	£90
Draping the balconies, and putting temporary floor to same and portico	£35
To clean and polish the granite columns on ground floor on North and East fronts, and clean the lamp standards	£17 10s. 0d.
To decorate the lamp standards with flowers (about)	£16
Fixing new device for illumination	£10
Illuminations	£150

These arrangements would not appear to have proved

wholly satisfactory to members, for on June 7th there was a further resolution to the effect "that Sherry, Light Claret, and Light Champagne should be supplied at 3s. 6d. per head, making the charge for the Luncheon 7s. instead of 3s. 6d. as previously arranged". Things were clearly going to be done on a bigger scale than had been originally intended, for on that same day the following estimates were approved:

11 Baskets of Flowers in Gas Stands	£5 15s. od.
11 Bands for above	£5 10s. od.
For staging inside the Coffee-Room and Morning-Room	£92
Addition to outside staging for seats	£12

As the great day approached further expenditure and regulations proved necessary. An extra estimate of £26–10–0 was passed for the erection of a platform at the east end of the Club to enable members to enter from the side street; while to ensure that there was no unseemly rush for seats an admonition was placed on the notice-board to the effect that "the Committee request that no Member will take seats on the staging either inside or out until all the Ladies are accommodated, and they have therefore reserved the upper part of the House solely for the use of Members. An entrance will be provided in the side street after 10.0 A.M." It was all very informal compared with the practice of more recent years.

In the Jubilee Honours the members of the Carlton fared well:

Earl
Londesborough
Peers of the United Kingdom
Viscount Galway
Earl of Strathmore

4. THE LIBRARY

Peerages

Sir James McGarel Hogg, M.P.

Right Hon. G. Sclater Booth, M.P.

Edward Fellowes, Esqr.

W. H. Eaton, Esqr., M.P.

Baronets

Sir A. Borthwick, M.P.

Charles Dalrymple, Esqr., M.P.

Col. Thursby

W. H. Houldsworth, Esqr., M.P.

C. E. G. Phillips, Esqr.

W. Pearce, Esqr., M.P.

R. Loder, Esqr.

F. Lucas, Esqr.

S. Cunliffe Lister, Esqr.

Privy Councillor

Right Hon. John Floyer

C.B.

Algernon Turnor, Esqr.

Henry Longley, Esqr.

Col. Henry Eyre

Col. R. P. Levine

Col. W. S. Stanhope

G.C.I.E.

Lord Connemara

Field-Marshal

The Earl of Lucan

As for the Club servants "in consideration of Her Majesty's Jubilee and the satisfactory manner in which the staff had performed their duties on the Jubilee Day, it was decided to grant each servant one week's pay".

It is interesting to compare the arrangements of 1887 with those that were made for the Diamond Jubilee ten years later; and on this second occasion the committee began to make their preparations rather longer in advance. The procession to St. Paul's, and the thanksgiving service on the steps of that cathedral, took place on June 22nd, but so early as March 16th the committee decided to ask the annual general meeting on the following day for permission "to invite distinguished visitors from India and the Colonies to become Honorary Members of the Club during their visit to England". This permission was readily granted, and honorary membership was in due course conferred upon the following:

Hon Wilfrid Laurier
Hon. Sir William Whiteway
Hon. G. H. Reid
Hon. C. C. Kingston
Hon. Sir John Forrest, K.C.M.G.
Hon. Richard John Seddon
Hon. Sir George Turner, K.C.M.G.
Hon. Sir Hugh Muir Nelson, K.C.M.G.
Hon. Sir Edward N. C. Braddon, K.C.M.G.
Hon. Sir J. Gordon Sprigg, K.C.M.G.
Hon. Harry Escombe
Hon. Thomas Byrnes
The Right Hon. S. J. Way
H.H. the Maharajah of Kapurthala
H.H. The Thakore Sahib of Morvi, K.C.I.E.
H.H. The Thakore Sahib of Gondal, K.C.I.E.
Maharaj Sir Pertab Singh, K.C.S.I., A.D.C. to the Prince of
    Wales
The Raja of Khetri
Colonel Lasseter
Sir Jamsetjee Jejeebhoy, Bt., C.I.E.
Hon. J. Gavan Duffy
Mr. Nowruz M. Parveez
C. de Soysa
Rai Bahadur Tip Narayan Singh

Presumably in the light of the experience gained at the Golden Jubilee the ladies' tickets, which were balloted for, were numbered and reserved, and no member was allotted more than one of these tickets, which cost a guinea each including luncheon. As before, the upper floor was reserved for members only. They were served with a fixed lunch which cost ten shillings a head including champagne, and temporary tables were placed in the coffee-room and the writing-room.

As to the cost of these festivities, an estimate was accepted of £250 for seating and £185 for decorations. In addition were the following items:

Staging on Smoking-Room balcony	£25
Granite pillars, flambeaux, etc., to be cleaned	£18
Window at end of Morning-Room to be made an entrance	£30

By this time the committee must have been quite accustomed to organizing festivities in connection with Royal processions. On June 23rd, 1891, it was resolved that "the same arrangements to be made for July 10th – the date of the German Emperor's visit to the City – as on the occasion of the visit of the Shah of Persia". These were that the ground-floor rooms should be opened to ladies, and the upper-floor reserved for members, while decorations were to be put up "at a cost of about £25". On July 6th, 1893, there took place the wedding of the Duke of York, later King George V, and Princess Mary of Teck, and the precedents set on the previous occasions were ordered to be closely followed.

In the main the committee adhered to the rule that guests should not be admitted to the Club except in the circumstances just described, and then the exception was only made in the case of ladies. There were, however, as has been shown on an earlier page, precedents for a relaxation of this custom, and they would appear to have governed the action of the committee on May 5th, 1893, for on that date "the Chairman (the Marquess of Abergavenny) made a proposal that a dinner should take place in the Club on June 7th, and that a certain number of gentlemen who were not Members of the Club should be invited. He urged this on political grounds, and stated that he had consulted the Leaders of the Party, who were strongly in favour of the suggestion". The proposal was adopted, and presumably the dinner took place.

Very different was the treatment meted out to the Pitt Club. In February, 1889, this eminently respectable dining club asked permission to hold a dinner at the Carlton, but only to be curtly informed that "the House Committee are unable to make exceptional arrangements for them, or give them greater facilities for a dinner than are enjoyed at present by Members of the Carlton Club". Exactly eleven years later the request was renewed when two letters were read from the secretary of the Pitt Club asking that a room at the Carlton Club might be allotted to the Pitt Club for a meeting. The secretary was directed to reply that under the rules "the Committee have not the power of taking the request into consideration". In view of the fact that only seven years before strangers had been allowed to dine in the Club, this answer was somewhat disingenuous; it is, however, satisfactory to know that in due course better relations between the two clubs were established, and since the installation of the annexe the Pitt Club has held many of its dinners at the Carlton.

With regard to what may be described as the purely internal affairs of the Club the closing years of the nineteenth century were peaceful, and the most notable event on the administrative side was another change of secretary in the summer of 1887. Mr. Chichester had only held the position for ten years, but on April 28th he asked for leave to go into the Middlesex Hospital for a month; the period had to be extended, and it is evidence of the friendly relations existing between the Carlton and the Junior Carlton that the following letter was sent to the secretary of the Junior Carlton:

Carlton Club,
Pall Mall, S.W.

April 26th, 1887

Dear Sir,

The Committee of this Club, having heard through Colonel Stracey that you have kindly offered to assist in the examination of the Club Accounts and business during the absence of Mr. Chichester, beg to thank you for your kind offer, which they are glad to accept.

The Committee have informed Mr. Chichester of your kind offer, and have instructed the Steward to give you every information and assistance in his power.

I remain,
yours faithfully,
Henry Fletcher,
Chairman, Sub-Committee.

Friendly co-operation between clubs could hardly go further.

Meanwhile it soon became obvious that Mr. Chichester would not be able to return to his duties, and the committee offered him a pension of £400 a year and honorary membership of the Club. This he accepted, and the following letter was thereupon sent to him:

Carlton Club,
July 26th, 1887.

My dear Chichester,

Your letter of yesterday has today been laid before the Committee, and I am instructed to convey to you how deeply they regret the cause of your resignation which under the circumstances they have felt bound to accept.

The Committee also desire me to express their sincere appreciation of, and best thanks for, the invaluable services rendered by you during the ten years you have held the office of Secretary, and to mark their sense of those services they unanimously decided to grant you a retiring allowance of £400 per annum, payable quarterly, and to take steps to confer upon you the Honorary Membership of the Club.

Believe me,

Yours very faithfully,

Chas. Martin[1],

Acting Secty.

This was much more generous treatment than his predecessors had received, and the ex-secretary replied:

Brighton,

July 27th, 1887.

My Lords and Gentlemen,

How to find words to express to you my gratitude for the high eulogium on my services which you have been pleased to use in conveying to me your Resolution granting me the large pension, and also for the honour you are about to confer on me, I know not, and I must ask you to believe me when I again repeat that it has grieved me to find my health has compelled me to resign so pleasant an office. However, your kindness and forbearance has softened the severance, and without doubt has greatly contributed to the present improvement in my health.

Thanking you again and again for the honour you propose conferring on me, and also for the generous manner in which you have considered my case throughout.

I have the honour to be

My Lords and Gentlemen,

Your faithful Servant,

C. M. S. Chichester.

---

[1] He was secretary of the Junior Carlton Club.

The minutes give a full account of the method by which the new secretary was chosen, and it is not uninteresting as evidence of the way in which an earlier generation handled these matters. First of all a special sub-committee was appointed to examine candidates, and to submit a short list to the Management Committee. This sub-committee then drew up the following advertisement:

The Secretaryship of the Carlton Club being vacant, the Committee are prepared to receive applications for the appointment stating age and forwarding copies of testimonials on or before the 1st of August next.

That was on July 27th, and the advertisement was inserted in four newspapers, namely *The Times, Morning Post, Daily Telegraph,* and *Standard.*

The total number of applications was 178, and this was reduced by the special sub-committee to seven, *viz.,*

> Colonel Atkinson
> Mr. Croft
> Hon. Otway Cuffe
> Mr. W. Hampton
> Mr. W. H. Rowe
> Mr. A. N. Streatfeild
> Mr. Cecil Tennant

Two of these seven, that is to say Atkinson and Hampton, withdrew, but the other five appeared before the House committee, and were then asked to appear in due course before the Management Committee, where the voting was as follows:

> A. N. Streatfeild   16
> J. D. Croft   3
> W. H. Rowe   3
> Hon. Otway Cuffe   2

Mr. Streatfeild thus became the fifth secretary of the Club, but there is no record of the terms upon which he was engaged. Unlike his predecessor, however, he did not have to wait until his retirement to be made an honorary member, for this privilege was accorded to him in 1898.

If the record of the Club for the last years of the nineteenth century in the main reflects the general prosperity and complacency which characterized that period, there is one aspect of its history at this time which throws an interesting light on the circumstances of some at any rate of the members, and that is the number of bankruptcies which were taking place. A typical year was 1895 when six members, of whom half were peers, were compelled to resign for that reason, and the figure remained fairly constant during the last decade of the nineteenth century. It was only after Mr. Streatfeild became secretary that the bankruptcy of members was noted in the minutes, so it is impossible to compare these figures with those of any earlier period, but they seem high for an era of such prosperity as the country had never previously known; and they would appear to show that not everybody, even in the upper classes, in that so-called age of privilege, found life easy. The custom, it may be added, seems to have been to reinstate a bankrupt member once he had obtained his discharge, though a good deal naturally depended upon the individual in question.

The installation of the telephone has already been chronicled on an earlier page, and in the spring of 1887 the question of lighting the Club by electricity began to be canvassed; a sub-committee was appointed to investigate the problem, and its report makes such interesting reading that it may, perhaps, be reproduced in full:

As a first step we availed ourselves of the courteous invitation of the Junior Carlton, Athenaeum, and Constitutional Clubs to inspect their various installations of the electric light and to see them in work.

We were supplied with a statement of their several costs.

We desire to place on record our sense of the kindness which we received in this matter from the committees of the above-mentioned clubs.

We made a careful inspection of the basement of this Club with a view to the possible adoption of an independent installation.

The present cost of lighting the Club is £1,360 per annum, there being 197 gas jets, a sunlight, and 92 lamps.

We invited and have received tenders for an independent installation from Messrs. Verity & Co., and from the Anglo-American Brush Coy.

We also invited and have received a tender from Sir Coutts Lindsay & Coy. for wiring the Club, and for the supply of lamps and electricity.

Your sub-committee feel unable to recommend the adoption of either of the tenders for independent installation, both because they can find no very convenient site for the necessary engine power, as well as because they think it advisable to await improvements which are foreshadowed.

They are of opinion that the estimate of Sir Coutts Lindsay & Coy. should be adopted and their tender accepted.

The expense of wiring and of lamps would have to be incurred in any case.

Should it be deemed expedient in the future to adopt an independent installation and supply by the use of gas or steam engines or batteries, the electricity given by Sir Coutts Lindsay & Coy. could be discontinued at three months' notice.

The estimate for wiring the Club and supplying 378 lamps giving the light of 6,200 candles is £848.

The annual renewals are estimated to cost about £160.

The electricity to be supplied at fixed rate of ¼d. per hour per lamp of 10 c.p. as measured by meter.

Your sub-committee consider that the total annual cost by this arrangement will not exceed £2,000 should all the 378 lamps be kept burning for 10 hours in each day of the year – a highly improbable contingency.

The sum is in excess of our present expenditure by £640. The excess, however, will be materially reduced by saving of labour in the lamp room, and in the less frequent necessity for cleaning and painting the Club.

We are of opinion that the electric light will considerably lessen the discomfort to Members by the present system of ventilation.

It is not intended to utilize the existing gas fittings, but they will remain available for gas lighting if necessary.

It was decided at a general meeting to adopt the recommendations of this report, and they were duly carried out in the manner described by the sub-committee in February of the following year:

My Lords and Gentlemen,

In view of the approaching Annual General Meeting of the Club, the committee appointed by you to deal with the question of lighting the Club House by electricity have the honour to lay the report of their proceedings on the table.

In the last report that your committee laid before you (April 28th, 1887) they stated that they had obtained tenders for the laying down a plant capable of generating a sufficient supply of current for their requirements, but that they thought it inadvisable at the present time to purchase machinery, They consequently recommended that the "wiring" of the Club should be undertaken at once, and that current should be taken from the mains of the Grosvenor Gallery, stating that should it be expedient in the future to adopt an independent installation, and supply by the use of gas or steam engines, or secondary batteries, the electricity taken from Sir Coutts Lindsay & Coy. could be discontinued at three months' notice.

Your committee were instructed to proceed on these lines, and a contract was entered into with Messrs. Thompson and Ritchie of Old Broad St. for the "wiring" and supply of the fitting and switches required.

The estimate that your committee reported to you was £1,200 – the amount of the contract was £1,197-2-4, including the fee (£40) to the consulting engineer.

The number of lights actually in use in the Club is:

On the basement and mezzanine – 112 lamps= 1,176 c.p.
On the upper floors   – 183 lamps= 3,156 c.p.
Making a total of 295 lamps giving 4,332 candle power.

In their previous report your committee mentioned as an outside cost the sum of £2,000 for current per annum, but they feel confident that the amount payable will be very much less as the lights are reduced from 378 to the present number.

The work was handed over by the contractors in good time and was ready at the time the Club re-opened on November 1st, 1887.

The meters were placed on the circuits from the outset, but it was found that owing to building operations the Converter Room was still very damp, and their action was impeded by rust, and they were removed. The walls are now dry, and they have been replaced, and are working satisfactorily.

Your committee think that a few more lights might be added with advantage in some parts of the building, while others might well be dispensed with. They would also suggest that the servants should be directed to turn off those lights which are not required. As this can be done so easily it is a pity to lose the advantage of the economy which would ensue.

Kintore.

As in many other instances in those early days of electricity the lighting was by no means always satisfactory, and hardly a month went by without some complaint on this score reaching the committee; indeed, on one occasion a return to gas was seriously considered. In the end, however, the difficulties were overcome.

Ten years later another amenity was introduced, and a lift was installed at a cost of £400. Its introduction would not appear to have caused any controversy, and it was unattended by such untoward incidents as those described on a later page which marked the installation of the lift at Arthur's.

On the subject of prices the minutes at this time are reticent, but there seems to have been a remarkable rise in the cost of coal. At any rate, in July 1893 the Club was paying 19s. 5d. a ton for the best Newcastle, which in July 1900 was costing 28s. 8d., while in the same period steam coal had risen from 17s. 9d. to 26s. 5d. As for food, the coffee-room prices were revised in the spring of 1896 in the following sense:

Fish to be limited to nine sorts.
Cold joints at lunch to be raised from 6d. to 9d.:
second helping 6d.
Pressed beef at lunch to be raised from 6d. to 9d.:
second helping 6d.
Ham – present price 1s. a plate and 6d. a slice to be altered to
9d. per portion.
Caviare to be raised from 6d. to 9d.
Chops to be raised from 6d. to 9d.
Steak – present price large 1s. 6d., small 1s.; to be altered to
1s. 3d. per portion.
Kidneys to be raised from 6d. for two to 8d. for two.
Omelette – present price large 1s., small 6d.; to be altered to
9d. each with two eggs.
Stilton cheese to be reduced from 6d. to 3d.

The only other allusion to coffee-room prices is in February 1889 when the price of poultry at dinner was reduced from 2s. 6d., and at lunch a second helping was to be 6d. instead of 1s.

Of references to the staff, and to the wages paid them,

there is singularly little. Of interest, however, is the entry on
May 25th, 1897, when the cook applied for an increase in his
wages – "It was decided that his wages should be increased to
£250 a year; that he should not be required to attend before
11.0 A.M.; and that he should be excused from attendance
every third Sunday, but that he should be held responsible
for the proper service of the kitchen during his absence."
These wages, it will be noticed, compare very favourably
with those paid fifty or sixty years before. On October 10th,
1899[1], the committee had for the first time to give a decision
on a matter with which their successors in 1914 and 1939 were
to be distressingly familiar – "The case of the carriage atten-
dant Wale, who was in the Army Reserve, was considered.
It was decided that his place should be kept open for him, and
7s. a week allowed to his wife while he was on active service."

The behaviour of the members seems to have been considerably less objectionable than in the earlier years of the
Club's history; not, however, that they did not make complaints, for there was hardly a meeting of the house committee
at which the secretary did not produce two or three lunch or
dinner bills backed with a complaint of some sort. Every
kind of criticism, request, and suggestion came before those
responsible for running the Club, as a few examples will serve
to show. On May 31st, 1887, there was a complaint from
Mr. Markham Spofforth "of the tarts served in the Club";
the matter was duly pondered, and instructions were given
"for larger tarts in future to be supplied". On March 13th,
1894, a letter was read from the Rev. T. Berney asking "that
the amount of a bet which he claimed to have won from
another member might be set off against his subscription",
which was surely an odd request to come from one of his

[1] The South African War began on the following day.

cloth: he was duly informed that "the Committee could take no action in the matter of the bet". More reasonable was the complaint of Mr. G. B. Napier on June 29th, 1897, "as to the number of mice in the dining-room". From time to time there is a faint echo in the minute books of events in the outside world, as on June 16th, 1891, when the secretary announced the resignation of Sir William Gordon Cumming, who had recently lost his action in connection with the famous game of baccarat at Tranby Croft.

The end of the long Victorian era saw the Club in a most flourishing condition. At the last meeting of the committee in the Queen's reign it was reported that the balance at the bank amounted to £21,488–8–9, and that there were 80 servants whose weekly board was 12s. 6d. each. During the previous week 156 dinners and 274 luncheons had been served, though in considering this figure it must be remembered that the month was January, when a good many members would not be in London; in a normal summer week about 200 dinners and 400 luncheons were the average. Furthermore, the number of those wishing to join the Club showed no sign of diminution. Candidates who were elected at the turn of the century had been on the waiting-list for seventeen or eighteen years, and it was accepted by the committee that men who put their names down in 1901 might have to wait twenty or thirty years. Members of either House of Parliament, of course, came up on a special list; among the new M.P.s returned at the general election of 1900, and elected to the Carlton in November of that year, occur the names of two future Prime Ministers, namely Winston S. Churchill and Andrew Bonar Law. In the following January the Queen died, and the Edwardian age began.

CHAPTER V

The Edwardian Era

IF the turn of the century found the Carlton in as strong a position as any committee could possibly expect both in respect of its finances and of its membership, the years which immediately lay ahead were difficult ones for the Conservative Party as a whole. The general election of 1900 had continued it in power with the handsome majority of 134 in the House of Commons, but in the summer of 1902 the Prime Minister, the Marquess of Salisbury, resigned, to be succeeded by his nephew, Arthur Balfour. This succession gave rise to difficulties which were to last for many years, and which caused the Conservative Party to lose three general elections in succession; for although Balfour had proved in the past, and was again to prove in the future, an admirable second-in-command, he was not a leader of men. In 1903 there occurred the great split on the subject of Tariff Reform, and all through the summer of that year the cleavage in the ranks of the Government's supporters grew more pronounced, while a delighted Opposition gleefully watched their enemies going through the same experience which they themselves had known seventeen years before when Gladstone had declared in favour of Home Rule.

Sir Michael Hicks-Beach, an ex-Chancellor of the Exchequer and a man whose opinion carried more weight than that of many a Cabinet Minister, came out against Joseph Chamberlain's Protectionist policy, and accused him of dividing his own party and of uniting the Liberals. This gave the signal for the formation of the Free Food League, which at its inception included no fewer than fifty-four Conservative and Unionist M.P.s, among them such young stalwarts as Lord Hugh Cecil, Major Seely, and Mr. Winston Churchill. On the other side the Tariff Reform League, largely owing to the efforts of Mr. Amery, was already in existence by the middle of June. Meanwhile dissension was not long in spreading from Westminster to the constituencies. No one knew what was the policy of the Government, and the rival organizations were canvassing for recruits among the members of the local associations.

By the time that the Cabinet met in the middle of September the Prime Minister had made up his mind to get rid of those who held strong views on the tariff question, whatever those views might be; he was determined to preserve unity if at all possible, even at the cost of losing some of his most valued colleagues. Accordingly Joseph Chamberlain (Colonial Secretary), C. T. Ritchie (Chancellor of the Exchequer), Lord George Hamilton (Secretary of State for India), Lord Balfour of Burleigh (Secretary for Scotland), and, after a brief delay, the Duke of Devonshire (Lord President of the Council) all resigned. Balfour, to quote a delightful phrase of Sir Sidney Lee in his *King Edward VII*, "was left with an indeterminate central body who for the moment followed his ambiguous lead of striving to steer between Chamberlain's Scylla and Ritchie's Charybdis".

Nemesis overtook the Balfour administration at the general election of 1906, when 134 Conservatives and 23 Liberal Unionists were returned to a House of Commons 670

strong.[1] This crushing defeat naturally affected the outlook of
the party which had suffered it, and during the long years from
1906 to 1914, when it seemed impossible for the Conservatives to get back to power, Tariff Reform appeared to many
of them to be a millstone round their necks, while dis-
heartened local leaders were heard to declare that Joseph
Chamberlain had wrecked two parties. It was such feelings
as these, it may be remarked in passing, that in the years
immediately before the First World War caused the larger
section of the Conservative Party to take up so enthusiasti-
cally the anti-Home Rule agitation as a policy more likely to
be a winning one than Tariff Reform.

The trials and tribulations of this period were reflected in
the history of the Carlton Club, and the committee continued
to pursue the same policy of restraint which had been adopted
by their predecessors sixty years earlier when the Party had
also been divided on the subject of tariffs – an attitude which,
as we have seen, was none too happily abandoned in the
'eighties by those who were responsible for the Club's
destinies at that time. It was not, however, always easy to
keep in the middle of the road.

In June 1904 the Hon. Ivor Guest, M.P. for Plymouth,
resigned, and in the following month Major Seely, M.P. for
the Isle of Wight, did the same thing; in April 1905 they were
joined by Mr. Winston Churchill.[2] The effect of the general
election of 1906 upon the Club can be gauged by the statistics
produced by the Chief Whip, Sir Alexander Acland-Hood,
to the committee in February 1906, which showed that three
months earlier there had been 283 M.P.s and 1,099 ordinary

[1] Some idea of the magnitude of this disaster can be gathered from a comparison
with the general election of 1945 when the Conservatives and their allies obtained
213 seats in a House of 640.
[2] He was re-elected in 1925.

members of the Club, whereas now the comparable figures were 93 and 1,285 respectively. The problem of what action, if any, should be taken in respect of those who split the Conservative vote soon arose again. Balfour had been defeated in Manchester at the general election, and the Hon. A. G. H. Gibbs, M.P. for the City of London, resigned so that his leader could return to Westminster. On February 20th, 1906, "Lord Hothfield drew attention to the fact that a Member of the Club, Mr. Thomas Gibson Bowles, was opposing Mr. Balfour at the election for the City of London", but "the subject having been discussed it was decided that no action should be taken at present". Bowles made no great showing at the poll, being defeated by Balfour by a majority of over eleven thousand in a straight fight, but the matter was not allowed to rest:

17.VII.1906.

Read a letter from the Hon. H. Bourke asking that Mr. T. Gibson Bowles should be requested by the Committee to withdraw from the Club.

The subject was discussed, and the Chairman[1] read a letter from Sir E. Carson stating that he considered the course suggested would be an unwise one.

It was proposed by Lord Ludlow, seconded by Col. Bagot, that a letter be written to Mr. Bourke stating that the Committee, having considered the matter, are unable to see their way to adopt the suggestion.

The proposal was put to the vote and carried, Viscount Ridley dissenting.

Gibson Bowles, it may be added, resigned at the end of the following year, but was reinstated in 1913, and subsequently served on the Library Committee.

[1] The 6th Marquess of Londonderry, K.G.

Then there was the curious case of H. H. Marks. He had been elected for the Isle of Thanet at a by-election in 1904, and retained the seat, though as an Independent Conservative, at the general election two years later. He was a newspaper proprietor by occupation, and was clearly an experienced politician for he had fought North-East Bethnal Green in 1892, and he had represented Tower Hamlets from 1895 to 1900. The objection to Marks seems to have been as much on personal as on political grounds, and that it was considerable and persistent there can be little doubt.

On December 20th, 1906, there was read "a letter from Lord Hugh Cecil calling attention to a report of the proceedings of the House of Commons in *The Times* of November 27th in regard to the personal character of Mr. H. H. Marks". The committee were not to be rushed, and Lord Hugh was merely told that his letter would receive their attention. In the middle of the following January the matter was taken a little further when a communication was produced from the Rev. H. Bull "with reference to a letter addressed to the Speaker of the House of Commons by sixteen electors of the Isle of Thanet making charges against Mr. H. Marks, M.P.". Once more the committee took no action, but merely acknowledged the reverend gentleman's letter. This answer was, apparently, far from satisfying Mr. Bull, who shortly afterwards wrote to ask if he was to expect any further reply, but he was informed that the committee had nothing to add. Lord Hugh Cecil then returned to the charge:

19.III.1907.

Read a letter from Lord Hugh Cecil again calling attention to the accusations made against Mr. H. Marks, M.P., and requesting the Committee to invite Mr. Marks to take proceedings to vindicate his character or retire from the Club.

The Secretary was directed to inform Lord Hugh Cecil that the Committee had decided to take no action in the matter.

Even this was not the end of the affair, for a letter arrived in due course from Lord Robert Cecil in support of his brother, but all to no purpose, for the committee refused to be moved.

Marks cannot have done anything very bad or the committee would have acted quickly enough, as was seen in the case of W. H. Cleland seven years later. He had been through the divorce court, and during the proceedings there Mr. Justice Bargrave Deane had reflected severely upon his conduct. When this was brought to the notice of the committee the secretary was instructed to write to Cleland in the following terms:

9th January, 1914.

Sir,

The attention of the Committee of the Carlton Club has been called to certain remarks made by Mr. Justice Bargrave Deane in delivering judgement in the suit of Cleland v. Cleland in the Divorce Court on the 6th day of December, 1913.

In the suit the Committee are informed you were the Respondent and that the remarks made by the learned Judge reflecting on the conduct of that party to the suit are applicable to you.

It is obvious to the Committee, as they think it must be to you, that reflections expressed by a learned Judge upon the Bench in reference to the conduct of one who is a Member of this Club cannot be passed by in silence, and without steps being taken of the kind contemplated by Rule XXX.

Before, however, proceeding to the extreme measure therein contemplated, the Committee desire me to say that they are willing to afford you any opportunity of impeaching the accuracy and justice of the observations made by the learned Judge, or if you are unable to do so, of resigning your Membership of the

Club. This for present purpose is the only object with which this letter is addressed to you.

Yours faithfully,
Walter H. Matthews,
Secretary.

W. H. Cleland, Esqr.,
  34 Brunswick Square,
    Hove, Sussex.

Cleland seems to have made some attempt to defend himself for "correspondence and interviews" with him were reported, but his explanations did not meet with the approval of the committee, with the result that when he put his resignation in their hands it was promptly accepted.

In the opening weeks of 1914 there was also an incident which recalls the behaviour of Sir John Cave in the earlier years of the Club:

5.II.1914.

The Committee having considered the inconveniences which were arising by reason of the fact that Col. Paget Mosley's health was such that he was guilty of proceedings which he would never have performed had he been in a normal condition of health and mind, the Secretary was instructed to write to Col. Mosley's Doctor and Solicitor saying that unless proper provision was made for his supervision and control, they will be under the painful necessity of removing his name from the Club, and instructing the servants not to permit his entry to the Club premises.

5.III.1914.

The Secretary reported letter written to the Solicitor and Doctor of Col. Paget Mosley in accordance with instructions of last meeting, and replies received thereto. The general position having been taken into consideration, the Committee, with regret, found themselves obliged to instruct the Secretary to see Col.

Mosley's Solicitor and inform him that unless he was able to report at the next meeting that Col. Mosley was not using the Club, they would have to take the necessary steps to have his name removed from the list of Members.

17.III.1914.

The Secretary reported steps taken in reference to Col. Paget Mosley, but that he was still using the Club. The Secretary was instructed to see Col. Mosley's Solicitor again, as in the opinion of the Committee it was impossible to allow this to continue.

Matters were not, however, to reach the climax which had marked the career of Sir John Cave, and no duke was to find Colonel Mosley deposited in a state of inebriety upon the doorstep of the Club in the early hours of a Sunday morning; instead, there are two brief allusions to the matter in the shape of further reports from the unfortunate member's solicitor and doctor, and thereafter silence.

To return, however, from the social to the political aberrations of the members during the early years of the twentieth century. A very curious case was that of Mr. W. M. Kavanagh, who had been returned at a by-election as Nationalist M.P. for County Carlow. On February 11th, 1908, a letter was read from him placing his resignation in the hands of the committee, but requesting that he might be allowed to remain a member of the Club on the condition that he did not use it until further notice. In retrospect it seems odd that a man who had been elected to further the cause of Home Rule should wish to belong to the club of a party one of the principal planks in whose platform was to oppose self-government for Ireland: this was the view taken by the committee, and Mr. Kavanagh's proferred resignation was immediately accepted.

Meanwhile events outside the walls of the Club were soon

to affect its internal affairs. The distinction between Conservatives and Liberal Unionists had with the passage of time become purely nominal, and defeat at the two general elections of 1910 caused both sections of the Opposition to do some hard thinking, with the result that they decided to amalgamate. In the autumn of 1911 Austen Chamberlain was elected a member, and during the next few weeks several other prominent Liberal Unionists followed him into the Club. On July 10th, 1912, it was officially decided that members of the Liberal Unionist Party should have the same privileges with regard to membership of the Club as were enjoyed by Conservatives.

Quite apart from the fact that the year 1912 was marked by a complete reorganization of the machinery of the Carlton it began to play a more prominent part in the activities of the Conservative Party than had been the case for a long time. This was in no small measure due to the influence of Walter Long which was dominant in the Club at that time and until his death in 1924. The rules regarding the eligibility of candidates were considerably tightened, and they now run as follows:

The Carlton Club is a Political Club designed to promote the principles and objects of the Conservative and Unionist Party. The only persons eligible for Membership are those who profess those principles and objects.

Each Candidate for admission must be proposed by one Member of the Club, and seconded by another; and the names both of the Candidate and of the Proposer and Seconder must be entered in the Book of Candidates. The Proposer and Seconder will be taken by such entry to vouch that the Candidate is a British Subject and belongs to the Conservative and Unionist Party, and that he recognizes this as the essential condition of his election to the Club. Any Member of the Club who ceases to be a Member of the Conservative and Unionist Party shall *ipso facto* cease to be a Member of the Club.[1]

It was also decided to revive the Political Committee, and a sub-committee was appointed to take the necessary steps to that end; how important this revival was considered is evident from the names of those who were selected to effect it:

> The Chairman of the Club
> Right Hon. Walter H. Long, M.P.
> Lord St. Audries
> Earl of Crawford and Balcarres
> Lord Edmund Talbot, M.P.
> H. D. Steel-Maitland, Esqr., M.P.
> Sir John Lonsdale, Bt., M.P.
> Almeric Paget, Esqr., M.P.
> Sir Douglas Straight
> Sir George Younger, Bt., M.P.

The suggested terms of reference were:

The Committee under no circumstances to initiate, or attempt to formulate, Party Politics; its objects and powers being limited to the promotion and furtherance of the interest of the Conservative and Unionist Party.

Objects. To back up, and assist in any way possible, the Party Whips and Party Organization. To help Party Organization by bringing it into closer touch with country districts and by "sitting on grousers". To encourage real Conservative principles in younger men of the Party by means of, *inter alia*, periodical Club dinners with Party guests.

Spheres of Action. To ascertain feeling in local districts. To find out people in their respective districts who will be useful as (a) Workers, (b) Subscribers, (c) Speakers. To assist the Central Organization by ascertaining suitable residents who are willing to

[1] Originally this rule only applied to those elected after October 1st, 1912, and the stipulation that a candidate must be a British subject did not exist.

entertain non-local Speakers. To look for, and obtain information as to, desirable Candidates for Parliament; desirable Candidates for election to Club. To obtain, and give, general information for use of Leaders of Party. To advise Leader of Party (through the Whips' room or the Party Organization) as to the real feelings throughout the districts with which they are connected on important matters.

Constitution. To be representative of the U.K. Zeal not the only qualification, but also judgement, tact, and experience. The Chairman of the Club to be Chairman of the Political Committee.

The sub-committee lost no time in getting to work, and on its recommendation the reconstituted Political Committee[1] came into existence in March 1914 with the following members:

> *Ex officio* – The Chairman of the Club
> Arbuthnot, Gerald
> Clinton, Lord
> Crawford and Balcarres, Earl of
> Fellowes, Right Hon. Ailwyn E.
> Kenyon, Lord, K.C.V.O.
> Lovat, Lord, K.C.V.O.
> Malmesbury, Earl of
> Paget, Almeric, M.P.
> St. Audries, Lord
> Straight, Sir Douglas
> Younger, Sir George, Bt., M.P.

Under this stimulus there was, as has already been noted, a marked revival in the political activities of the Club, and considerable sums of money were raised for the fight against Home Rule. Nor was this all, for the recommendation to encourage the younger members of the Party was carried out, and in particular valuable assistance was given to the undergraduate Conservative clubs at Oxford.

[1] The Political Committee lapsed in the twenties, and was revived a few years after the Second World War.

The years which immediately preceded the First World War constituted a period of fierce party strife, and that, in these circumstances, some tightening of the Club's rules in respect of the political opinions of the members was necessary is proved by the case of J. C. S. Rashleigh, which in some ways was even more extraordinary than that of W. M. Kavanagh. On February 5th, 1914, there was brought before the committee some correspondence which had passed between the Secretary and Rashleigh, "in which he (i.e. Rashleigh) stated that since the autumn of 1909 he had been supporting the Liberal side, and contended that there was nothing in the Rules to prevent his continuing to do so, and at the same time retaining his Membership of the Club". He stressed the fact that the new rule only applied to members elected after October 1st, 1912, and he went on to say that in December, 1909, he had been informed by the then secretary[1] that he could retain his membership if he wished.

It requires no great effort of imagination to picture the effect created by this letter upon the committee at a time of acute political tension, and the secretary was instructed to write to Rashleigh in the following terms:

6th February, 1914.

Dear Sir,

Referring to your letter of the 22nd ult., I am instructed by my Committee to point out that this Club was from its institution a Conservative Club, and that it was a matter of common knowledge that the holding of Conservative views was an essential qualification of Membership. Owing to the fusion which of recent years has taken place between the old Conservative and Liberal Unionist Parties, Resolutions were passed in 1912 under which persons supporting the "Conservative and Unionist Party" were admitted to Membership, thus accounting for the wording of the Rule to which you call attention.

[1] A. N. Streatfeild.

My Committee are surprised at the information you have given them in reference to the interview with the late Secretary in 1909, and I am instructed to inform you that they cannot accept the views therein expressed, as, whilst not suggesting that it is their duty to take official cognisance of the views which individual Members may take on some particular question of policy, they are unanimously of opinion that it was, at the date of your said interview and is now, injurious to, and inconsistent with, the character and interests of the Club that one of its Members should be persistently "supporting the Liberal side", and that the more so is this the case where such Member is, like yourself, a man of position and influence in his locality, taking an active interest in politics.

I have consequently to inform you that unless you have resigned your Membership of the Club before the 5th of March next, the Committee will be obliged to take the necessary steps to put in force the provisions of Rule XXX.

Yours faithfully,
Walter H. Matthews,
Secretary.

J. C. S. Rashleigh, Esqr.,
Throwleigh, Okehampton.

Rashleigh did not see the matter in quite this light, and he maintained his right to support the Liberal Party while remaining a member of the Club; however, he was willing to resign if his entrance fee and one year's subscription were returned to him. The committee duly considered this offer, and replied that the subscription would be refunded, but not the entrance fee. Rashleigh apparently ignored this suggestion, for a special general meeting was held on May 5th "to consider whether or not the conduct of Mr. J. C. S. Rashleigh, of Throwleigh, Okehampton, has been injurious to, or inconsistent with, the character or interests of the Club. If yea, whether or not his name should be removed from the Club.

The allegation against said Member was that he is, and has been since the autumn of 1909, actively and publicly supporting the Liberal side".

The official report of the subsequent proceedings is brief:

In the absence of Mr. Rashleigh, who had notice of the meeting but was not in attendance, the whole of the correspondence which had passed between Mr. Rashleigh and the Secretary, in which Mr. Rashleigh admitted that since the autumn of 1909 he had given his support to the Liberal side, having been considered, the Members present were unanimously of opinion that such conduct was injurious to, and inconsistent with, the character and interests of the Club, and it was accordingly proposed by the Chairman and seconded by the Right Hon. Walter H. Long, M.P. and carried unanimously, That Mr. J. C. S. Rashleigh's name be removed from the Club.

This is, it may be remarked, the only recorded instance of a member being expelled from the Club.

How strong party feeling was at this time may be gauged from a suggestion made in the spring of 1912 by a member, C. Stewart, that "the Union Jack should be kept flying on the roof until the Home Rule Bill were defeated or withdrawn"; this proposal did not, however, commend itself to the committee. Two months earlier the same member had raised the question of his son Bertrand, who was "confined in a German fortress[1]". In consequence, it was decided to put his son's name on the Abroad List.

Before passing from the political to the social activities of the Club during the opening years of the nineteenth century

[1] Bertrand Stewart was convicted at Leipsic in February 1912 on a charge of "attempted betrayal of military secrets", and was sentenced to three and a half years' imprisonment in a fortress. He obtained information from a professional Belgian spy of doubtful character about certain fortifications on the North Sea coast and the disposition of German ships in connection with them, but he had been unable to get his information through to the Admiralty.

it is pleasant to record the friendliness which was displayed by the committee towards the 1900 Club from its inception. The 1900 Club was founded in March 1906 by a number of those who had sat in the 1900 Parliament, but its membership was almost at once much more widely extended, and it has ever since played an influential part in the counsels of the Conservative Party. On March 19th, 1907, "the Secretary was directed to put up a notice of the Dinner of the 1900 Club to the Colonial Premiers, inviting applications from Members for tickets up to March 30th". This instruction created a precedent, for it was the first time that an announcement had appeared on the Carlton notice-board which did not refer to some activity of the Club, and ever since only the announcements of the meetings of the 1900 Club have been allowed to be put up in this way. Incidentally, this 1900 Club Dinner to the Colonial Premiers was one of the largest ever to be held in London: it took place in the Albert Hall, and some idea of its scope can be gathered from the fact that among the refreshments for the 1,600 diners there were ordered:

Beef for soup (lbs.)	4,500	Champagne, bottles	1,400
Whole Salmon	200	Hock, bottles	1,500
Quails	2,500	Liqueur brandy, bottles	300
Asparagus (sticks)	25,000	Chartreuse, bottles	300
Fresh strawberries (lbs.)	600	Creme de Menthe, bottles	500
		Whisky, bottles	200

There were five hundred cooks and waiters, and the total cost was £4,000.

A more modest repast on the part of the 1900 Club was envisaged in the minutes some eighteen months later:

15.XII.1908.

Colonel Lockwood stated that Members of the 1900 Club who

belong to this Club had expressed a wish to dine together here. It was decided that the Committee Room might be used for this purpose, or if a larger number than twelve wished to dine arrangements should be made in the Coffee-Room for the purpose.

These years were marked by two coronations, and the Club's arrangements followed very closely the precedents set at the Diamond Jubilee of Queen Victoria. The postponement of the coronation of King Edward VII resulted in considerable inconvenience, but the actual financial loss was reduced to a minimum by the simple expedient of only returning part of the money paid for tickets. By the coronation of King George V prices and standards had risen considerably, as is shown by the following entry:

7.II.1911.

That 161 seats should be built out on the ground floor facing Pall Mall for ladies as in 1902. That Ladies' tickets should be balloted for; the first 161 numbers to be for the first day, and the rest for the second day.[1] £3-3-0 to be charged for each Lady's ticket to include luncheon and light refreshments for the Lady only.[2]

This represented a considerable advance on the ten shillings charged for lunch on the occasion of the Golden Jubilee.

A number of honorary members were elected from among distinguished overseas visitors, and this procedure was also adopted at the coronations of King George VI and Queen Elizabeth II, though on the latter occasion hospitality was naturally on a more reduced scale as the Club was in less commodious premises at 69 St. James's Street.

As we have seen, the years 1912 and 1913 were marked by

[1] There was a march-past of some 50,000 British, Indian, and Colonial troops under the command of Lord Kitchener on the day after the Coronation.
[2] For the Coronation of Queen Elizabeth II the price was £15 15s. including breakfast, champagne lunch, and tea.

a number of changes in the administration of the Club, and the machinery then established has been retained virtually intact to this day. The Political Committee was revived, and for the first time there was a chairman of the Club, in the person of Lord Claud Hamilton; the committee was also reduced in numbers, and in future a certain number of its members were to retire in rotation. As on previous occasions when administrative reforms took place there was a change of secretary, and in 1912 A. N. Streatfeild gave place to Walter H. Matthews. For purposes of comparison it may be noted that the retiring secretary was voted a pension of £500 a year, and his successor was appointed at a salary of a like sum.

The First World War, a turning-point not only in the life of the Club but in the history of mankind, was now approaching, and a brief review of the position of the Club as the shadows began to lengthen may not be out of place. As a result of the reorganization a number of memoranda were prepared at this period which provide just the required information.

First, as regards membership. On February 5th, 1914, the following report was submitted to the Committee on this matter:

There are 101 Candidates to be elected during 1914 to bring the number of Ordinary Members up to the total authorized by the Rules, *viz.*, 1,500.

During 1913 there were elected slightly more Members than twice the average annual election, but to obtain this number Candidates had to be taken from entries extending over a period of 14 years, *i.e.* from 1896 to 1910. The reason for this appears to be that the bulk of Candidates entered for early selection and election, and younger sons or relations of Members, who, when their turn arrived, were not of age or desirous of taking up election.

The result is that further elections during the current year must very largely be from Candidates entered during the year 1911 and subsequently.

There are only 57 Candidates awaiting election who were entered in 1911, and 61 who were entered in 1912, and if the same proportion applies to this year as applied to the previous years, not more than one in three of these will desire to take election, but probably owing to the more recent date of entry a greater proportion will take election.

During 1913, the Candidates entered in the Ordinary List represented about the average annual shrinkage without taking into consideration deaths and other casualties in this list before their turn for Ballot arrives, but in addition to these Ordinary entries, there were 54 Candidates entered in earlier years, who, on their turn for Ballot arriving, asked to have their names left, and have been re-entered at the bottom of the list.

In addition to the above, there are 306 Candidates who were entered prior to 1911, but whose elections are standing over for various reasons or from whom no reply can be obtained.

From this it would seem to follow that the membership position was not so good as it had been fourteen years earlier, and that even if the First World War had not taken place it might in due course have become difficult.

As to finance, no figures are available after the reorganization in 1912 when a Finance Committee came into being; presumably the relevant statistics were laid before it, and not, as previously, before the Committee of Management, but its minutes have not survived. The last reference to finance was on July 16th, 1912, when it was reported that the balance at the bank amounted to £23,484 0s. 6d., and that there were eighty-two servants whose weekly board was 12s. 6d. each,

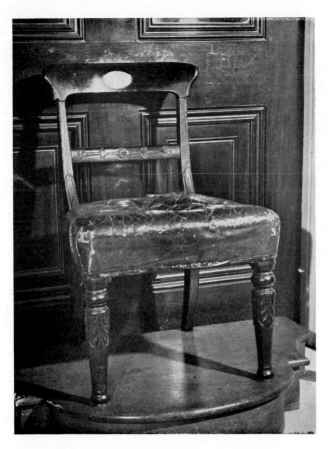

5. LORD BEACONSFIELD'S CHAIR

and that during the previous week 166 dinners and 378 luncheons had been served. This showed a state of affairs comparable with that at the turn of the century, though there would appear to have been a slight diminution in the number of members dining, possibly because more M.P.s were taking their dinner at the House of Commons.

With regard to the tastes of the members, there is a memorandum of the Wine Committee, dated March 6th, 1913, relating to the consumption of port, and a few extracts from it are enlightening:

The Wine Committee beg to report that, on January 1st, this year, the stock of Vintage Ports of or prior to 1904 consisted of 3,440 bottles and 1,575 half-bottles – equalling 4,228 bottles.

The consumption of Vintage Ports has of late been steadily increasing; last year it amounted to 822 bottles, so that at the present rate of consumption these Vintage wines would be finished during 1918.

There are no first-class Vintage Ports between 1904 and 1908, and the wines of the latter year are not likely to be ripe for drinking before 1920, so that there is an interval of from two to three years to be provided for. In other words, there is a shortage in the stock of Vintage Port of or prior to 1904 of about 175 dozen. Good wines of these Vintages will cost from 75s. to 115s. per dozen, so that calculated at 84s. per dozen, the total cost of making up the shortage would be £735.

In order to avoid a repetition of the present shortage it will be necessary to purchase sufficient Port of 1908 Vintage to last until the 1912 wines are ready for drinking. This will probably not be before 1925, so that at least five years' consumption of 1908 Ports should be purchased, that is to say 350. The Club at present has 115 dozen, of which 58 dozen are Cockburn's shipping and 57 Dows's.

The last pre-war meeting of the committee was held on July 30th, 1914, when the usual arrangements for the annual closing were announced, and it was decided that the committee should meet again on November 5th. It actually met on the following Sunday, August 2nd, to deal with the case of those members of the staff who had been recalled to the Colours.

CHAPTER VI

The Carlton Club Meetings

THERE have been two occasions in the present century when the name of the Carlton Club has come prominently before the British public: the first was in 1911 when at a meeting held there Bonar Law was elected leader of the Conservative Party, and the second was in 1922 when the decision was taken no longer to support Lloyd George and his coalition administration. In view of the attention they attracted both events call for extended notice in any history of the Club.

In consequence of the differences of opinion in the Party as to the attitude to be adopted towards the Parliament Bill in the summer of 1911 Balfour's position as leader became increasingly difficult, quite apart from the growing influence of a school of thought which held that the time had come to replace a man who had led his followers to defeat at three successive general elections. Such being the case it was small wonder that the three letters B.M.G. – Balfour Must Go – began to make their appearance in the Press, while each day it became more obvious that the Opposition was so divided as to be incapable of making any effective resistance to the Government. During the early autumn there had been repeated rumours that Balfour was contemplating resignation, but at the end of October they took on a more definite form, and during the opening days of the following month some at least of his colleagues on the front bench were informed that they were true. The secret was, however, confined to a very small circle, and the Party as a whole was quite unprepared for the announcement when Balfour made it on the afternoon of Wednesday, November 8th, to his constituents of the City of London.

At this point it may be as well to explain exactly what was at issue. Balfour had, as we have seen, in 1902 succeeded his uncle, the third Marquess of Salisbury, as leader of the Party as a whole, but whoever was now chosen to follow him would only be leader in the Commons. It was still possible, not only constitutionally but practically, for a Prime Minister to be in the Lords – only nine years had elapsed since such had been the case – and it would not be until the Party returned to power that it could be seen for whom the Sovereign would send; this individual would then be elected leader of the whole Party, whether he were a peer or a commoner. In the meantime Lansdowne would continue to lead in the Upper House, and whoever succeeded Balfour would lead in the Lower. The fact that the Party was in Opposition also settled the place of meeting to decide the question. Parties in office had been in the habit of meeting at the Foreign Office in similar circumstances in the past, but in the present instance the Carlton Club was clearly indicated.

From the beginning there could be no doubt that the two principal candidates for the vacant leadership would be Austen Chamberlain and Walter Long. Austen seems to have known of Balfour's intentions as early as November 4th, and he has left on record his diagnosis of the situation as he saw it at that time. "I think it is true to say that my colleagues in the late government, including the Whips, the keener Tariff Reformers, and many of the younger men, thought that I was the better fitted to fill the vacancy, but I still called myself a Liberal Unionist, I had only joined the Carlton Club a little time before, and the part which I had taken in recent events had certainly aroused some passing antagonism. Long, on the other hand, was a life-time Conservative, a typical country gentleman, and senior to me both in length of service in the House and in Cabinet rank, and he aroused none of the jealousies or doubts which were inseparable from my position." Austen's candidature was, in particular, strongly supported by Lord Winterton, Mr. Waldorf Astor (later Viscount Astor), Mr. Arthur Lee (later Viscount Lee of Fareham), Mr. (later Sir) C. E. Warde, Mr. (later Sir) Laming Worthington-Evans, and Mr. Bertram Falle (later Lord Portsea).

Austen would have been less than human had he been altogether unmoved at the prospect of becoming Balfour's successor, but he regarded it with at least as much apprehension as hope. "I wish", he wrote, "there were another Balfour, clearly superior to us, and obviously marked out for the post. How gladly would I play second fiddle to him. But there is no such man at present, and having given my life to this work and got to the position I now hold, I cannot shirk fresh responsibilities or heavier burdens if they fall to my lot." Exasperating as he had often found Balfour, and frequent as had been his disagreements with him, he entertained a very genuine affection for the older man, and regret at his retirement was not unmixed with sorrow that his own activities in connection with the Halsbury Club might possibly have precipitated Balfour's decision.

Long does not seem to have heard of his leader's intentions until Monday the 6th, possibly he was at Rood Ashton for the weekend, but they were not unexpected by him, even if the moment chosen took him by surprise. A week earlier there had been a meeting at Devonshire House of which Long was one of the organizers, attended by some of Balfour's friends, to discuss the best way to strengthen his position as leader; at this meeting Lord Derby and Alfred Lyttelton had stated as their opinion that Balfour's resignation might be anticipated at no very distant date, but neither of them believed that it would take place soon, or that their leader had absolutely made up his mind. "Consequently", Long has left it upon record, "the announcement made by Sandars[1] that A. J. B. had made up his mind to resign, that he was going to announce the fact to a meeting of his constituents on the following Friday, and that a meeting was to be called to select his successor on the following Monday, was to me a staggering blow. I had served under Balfour for more than twenty years; I had stood resolutely by him during recent years when his leadership had been vigorously assailed by members of his own Party; I had done my best to strengthen his position and secure the continuance of his leadership; and to be suddenly told, without any real warning, that he had decided, without any sort of preparation for his Party, to resign immediately, was naturally an event of the most serious and trying kind".

Although he had supported the official policy over the Parliament Bill, and had refrained from joining the Halsbury Club, Walter Long was not at that moment in his leader's good books, as he himself fully realized. Like his rival he had experienced the discontent with Balfour which was widespread in the Conservative Party, and at the end of September he had sent the leader a memorandum in which he out-

[1] The Right Hon. J. S. Sandars, Private Secretary to Balfour when Prime Minister.

lined the position as he saw it. Balfour had already come to
the conclusion that his successor in the Commons should be
Austen, so it would be incorrect to say that this memorandum
was the cause of his opposition to Long's election, but it
certainly served to stiffen his attitude to his candidature, for
he resented the document quite considerably. Lord Balcarres
shared Balfour's feelings, as Long was fully aware, for he
wrote: "It was evident to me that Lord Balcarres, the Head
Whip of the Party, was strongly of opinion that Mr.
Chamberlain ought to be made leader, and I attributed his
view very largely to the fact that he was at Balmoral when
my letter arrived, that he had probably seen it and resented
my action, and felt that as I had had something to do with
Mr. Balfour's retirement I ought not to follow him. In
addition, I believe he was of opinion, no doubt rightly, that
Mr. Chamberlain would make a better successor than I."
Long was correct as to the attitude of the Chief Whip, who
had said a fortnight before, "Well, if I have anything to do
with it, I don't mean the Party to have Long for leader."

It was Lord Helmsley, subsequently second Earl of Fever-
sham, then representing Thirsk and Malton, who persuaded
Long to allow his name to go forward for the vacant leadership, and among his supporters were Sir William Bull, Sir
Harry Samuel, Mr. (later Sir) Ian Malcolm, Lord Charles
Beresford, Lord Castlereagh (later Marquess of Londonderry), Sir W. R. Anson, Mr. George Terrell, Mr. Jessel
(later Lord Jessel), Mr. Charles Bathurst (later Lord Bledisloe),
and Mr. E. Fitzroy (later Speaker of the House of Commons).
Long was by no means eager to be nominated, for he has
left it on record that he greatly doubted his own powers, and
he was not at all sure that his health would stand the strain
to which it would necessarily be subjected. On political

grounds he was equally reluctant to enter the lists against Austen Chamberlain, for he felt strongly "that we owed so much to his father that it would be proper to pay him the tribute of electing his son". Nevertheless, his friends persuaded him to stand, alleging that if he gave way to his rival there was a strong section which would not follow a Liberal Unionist.

Of the prospects of the two men it is difficult to speak with any certainty, but the probability is that Long would have carried the day. Lord Curzon expressed the view at the time that this would be the case, and a careful canvass by Samuel and Bull showed a majority of seventy for Long. On the other side Balcarres told Austen that he "could not say which would get a majority". One back bencher, who subsequently attained Cabinet rank, wrote a letter marked "Strictly Confidential" both to Austen and to Long promising his vote.

The secret of Balfour's resignation was well kept from the world at large until the afternoon of November 8th, when he himself announced it to his constituents. Almost at the same hour his two potential successors, together with Henry Chaplin, met accidentally at the House of Commons, having arrived simultaneously at the Ladies' Gallery entrance. They at once adjourned to Balfour's room to discuss the situation. After some preliminary conversation Austen stated his case. It was evident, he said, that the respective friends of Long and himself intended to run them for the leadership; that there was so far no sign of any other candidate; but that it was more than probable that other candidates would be forthcoming. He went on to say that in his opinion it was impossible either for Long or himself to withdraw, since such an act would only be regarded as a betrayal by their respective friends, and would result in great bitterness and strife.

All the same, in the event of a third candidate upon whom everybody could agree coming forward, he would suggest that they should both retire in favour of this third individual. Long readily agreed with this, and the decision was communicated to the Chief Whip.

The following day, Thursday the 9th, was not a happy one for either of the protagonists. The lobbies at Westminster and the smoking-room of the Carlton Club were the scenes of an agitation which increased with every passing hour as the groups of excited partisans became more heated. Long, it was declared by Austen's supporters, was the representative of a Toryism that had had its day, and in any case he would be quite useless as a leader; to this it was replied with some heat that Austen was not a Conservative at all, that he was a nonconformist, and that if he were chosen the Party would be run by the Birmingham caucus. In these circumstances it is not surprising that the principals should have come to view each other with a certain amount of suspicion, for the more violent of their followers did all that was possible to poison their minds against one another. For example, on the Friday Chamberlain received the following letter from his opponent:

Written last night, but omitted to post it.

65 Eaton Square, S.W.

My dear Austen,

This is d——le ! I have heard two statements today. First, that you and I have had a long and unending feud; second, that I would not "serve under you". I hope I need not say that there is no more foundation for the last than you know as well as I do there is for the first.

Yours ever,
Walter H. Long.

9.XI.11.

At first it seemed probable that the third candidate would be Carson, but he refused to allow his name to go forward; on the Thursday evening, however, Bonar Law entered the field, sponsored by E. A. Goulding, later Lord Wargrave, and Austen and Long both withdrew in his favour. On Monday, the 13th, the fateful meeting was held at the Carlton Club to choose a leader in the House of Commons, and there were 232 Members of Parliament present. It was, curiously enough, the first time that Austen had set foot in the building, for, as we have seen, it was but recently that he had been elected, since Liberal Unionists had not hitherto been eligible for membership. On the proposal of Lord Claud Hamilton, seconded by Colonel Lockwood, Chaplin was voted into the chair, and Long then moved the election of Bonar Law to fill the place of Balfour. He began by paying a tribute to the work of Balcarres during the previous week, and after saying that Austen and himself had worked in close agreement in the last few days, he went on to deal with the merits of Bonar Law. Long finished on a note which some of those present must have thought strange coming from him:

I believe it has been a drawback to our Party that we have seemed to be always identified in our high posts with the land. Now, we have an opportunity which may never recur, my lords and gentlemen, if we do not take it. We have a chance of saying to our political opponents who are jeering at us, who are going about saying, as one of them said the other day, that we are all scrambling for the mantle which our great leader has laid down – we can answer them by saying in the clearest way: "There is no scramble; the Party is absolutely united." No man is fighting for this great honour; we are all agreed; and we are going today to hand the mantle to a man in whom we have confidence . . . and a man who has been trained in the best of business circles. As a real business man he will bring to our councils, to the conduct of our debates, to the management of our business the mind of a business-man above and beyond all other things.

Long spoke for twenty-five minutes, and his speech was generally considered to be, both in manner and matter, one of the best he ever made.

Austen then rose to second the resolution, and began by saying, "Mr. Long said he spoke for himself, but, indeed, he spoke for me too. I agree with every word that he has said. I have nothing to do now except to support the proposal that he has made, and to urge it upon your acceptance. I know, of course, that, as he said, there has been a little feeling that the matter has been taken out of the hands of the Party, and too much settled for you before you came to this gathering." Some murmurs of "Hear, hear" at this point showed that he had not misinterpreted the feelings of his audience on this score, so he continued: "Now, if there be any feeling of that kind, I think the best way to meet it, and the best answer I can give to it, is to tell you in the simplest possible terms what has happened as I know it."

He then gave an abstract of the events of the Wednesday, Thursday, and Friday of the previous week, finishing with these words:

We felt, as everybody must feel in such circumstances, that though to be leader of a great Party like this in the House of Commons is a post that no man would decline without some regrets, and that anyone might be very proud to occupy, no personal question could be permitted to interfere with the great interests of the Party and the cause for which it stands. Mr. Long very properly said that we have never talked about claims. No man had claims upon the Party except as he could serve the Party and as his nomination would be in its best interests. What we did talk about was whether our names should go forward or not.

We thought they ought to go forward, in the first instance, in order that it might be seen whether the Party clearly preferred any one of us. We thought that they ought to be withdrawn when we saw that there was no such clear consensus of opinion in the Party, and when it became evident that it would be much easier for his friends and for my friends, and I think I may frankly say for him and for me (Mr. Walter Long: Hear, hear), as well as for our friends, to give our full, our hearty, and our cordial support to Mr. Bonar Law than it would be for the friends of either of us to give all the support that was necessary to the other, chosen in such circumstances as I have described.

Austen concluded with an appeal for loyalty to the new leader:

Mr. Bonar Law, if he be your choice, is not to be envied, but neither is he to be pitied. You give him a great opportunity, to the height of which I believe he will rise; but if you give him that opportunity you have got to give him your whole heart. You have got to do it in no grudging spirit. There must be no regrets and no questionings left behind. The man who takes that position needs the united support of a united Party. The position is intolerable on any other terms, and, as we definitely withdraw our names, as Sir Edward Carson's name is withdrawn, we ask you not merely to make your decision a unanimous one today, but to pledge yourselves to give him that whole-hearted support without which neither he nor any leader can do justice to himself, nor successfully conduct the affairs of a great Party.

The meeting then proceeded to elect Bonar Law, and after a few words of thanks from the new leader it broke up. As Bonar Law was leaving the room a back bencher came up to him, and congratulated him. The M.P. then went on, "You're not very well known to our fellows, and you must get yourself popular. What you want to do is to drink a bottle of Champagne a day, and look as if you did."

The ensuing years, first of bitter party strife and then of

the First World War, were marked by considerable political activity in the Club, a fact to which the two volumes of *The Apologia of an Imperialist* by W. A. S. Hewins bear witness. Hewins was a frequenter of the Club, and he served on the Library Committee for a number of years. He was Member of Parliament for the City of Hereford from 1912 to 1918, and he was Under-Secretary for the Colonies from 1917 to 1919. A few quotations from his autobiography will serve to show the importance of the Club at that period as a meeting-place of the more active members of the Party.

On May 26th, 1915, there was a Party meeting at the Club, apparently to consider the composition of the First Coalition which had just come into office, and of this Hewins wrote, "The meeting at the Carlton Club was not very fully attended. No doubt the notice was short. The meeting was, I will not say, against the new ministry, but certainly not in favour of it, doubtful and uneasy. The prevailing opinion was that the ministry in its present form would last from six weeks to three months. Members of the Business Committee were in favour of criticism as before." There was another meeting at the Club on July 7th, 1916. "The party meeting at the Carlton Club yesterday was well attended," wrote Hewins, "considering there were so many of our men serving. The speeches of ministers justified the Hardinge report. They were just old stuff, and showed no knowledge or appreciation of the situation in Ireland or anywhere else."

In addition to formal gatherings of this nature the Club was an unofficial meeting-place for members of the Party in and out of office. In September 1919 there was a railway strike, and Hewins is found noting in his diary, "I discussed the whole situation at and after lunch with my friends at the Carlton Club". The Conservative leaders of those days were

always about the Club, and prominent in this connection
was Walter Long who was for a time Hewins' chief at the
Colonial Office. Long was a stalwart supporter of the Club,
and whenever the House of Commons rose sufficiently early
to allow him to do so he always looked in at the Carlton on
his way home from Westminster. Bonar Law and Austen
Chamberlain were often in the Club, while Balfour, on the
other hand, was rarely to be found there. He was never much
of a man for clubs, but when he was Prime Minister he was
persuaded by J. S. Sandars to look in at the Carlton late one
evening; unfortunately, there were very few members in the
building, and he rarely entered it afterwards, apparently
because he did not think it worth the trouble.

In 1921 there was another meeting at the Club to elect a
leader of the Party in the House of Commons, and for a brief
space it seemed as if the verdict of ten years before had been
set aside. Bonar Law had not been in good health for some
time, and in March he was compelled to give up all public
work. There was only one possible successor, and that was
Austen Chamberlain, who accordingly became Lord Privy
Seal and Leader of the House of Commons. No other name
was seriously considered, though mention was made of
Sir Robert Horne in some quarters. Yet the prize was not so
attractive as it had seemed a decade earlier, and Austen
accepted it as much from a sense of duty as for any other
reason:

Ten years ago I thought I should be chosen leader of the Party,
and resigned my chances not without regret to a man only a year
or two older than myself and very much my junior in the House
of Commons. It never occurred to me then or since that the chance
would come to me again, and though Bonar Law has often complained of being very tired, I thought him at least as good a "life"

whether political or otherwise as my own. And now he falls out so suddenly and unexpectedly that it leaves us all sad and breathless, and the wheel of fortune turning full cycle brings to me again what ten years ago I should have liked, and what I now accept as an obvious duty, but without pleasure or any great expectations except of trouble and hard labour. . . . As one after another of one's old colleagues drops out of the ranks I feel sad and lonely, and do not experience as of old the joy and fire of battle.

Austen could, indeed, hardly have become leader at a more unfortunate moment, and it was a most uneasy inheritance upon which he now entered. The Conservative Party was in office, it is true, but as a partner in a Coalition that was every day becoming more unpopular in the country as the by-elections were abundantly proving. There was no opportunity of initiating policy, and all that could be done, in view of the widespread economic and social unrest, which seemed to grow worse instead of better, was to work away at the liquidation of the war. All this was bad enough, but those whom Austen was to lead were themselves becoming every day more divided. "Members have been growing increasingly restive in the House", he wrote, and this was no exaggeration. Such was the legacy which Bonar Law bequeathed to his successor.

Nevertheless, Austen's start was promising. "The Party meeting," he said, "was very cordial, and gave me a great reception." It was held at the Club on March 21st, and Lord Edmund Talbot was in the chair. Messages in favour of Austen as leader of the Party in the House of Commons were read from Balfour, Long, Carson, and Horne, and a resolution to this effect was proposed by Captain Pretyman and seconded by Sir Edward Coates. It was carried unanimously, and Austen then entered the room to the accompaniment of continued cheers. His speech was a short one, but after paying a tribute to the memory of his predecessor he took the opportunity of reminding his hearers of his attitude towards the Coalition:

I am not going here and now to attempt to forecast the future of our Party or even of the Coalition; but there are moments when insistence upon Party is as unforgivable as insistence upon personal things, when the difficulties which the nation has to confront call for a wider outlook and a broader union than any that can be found even within the limits of a single party, and when the traditions of more than one party, the ideas of more than one party, need to be put into the common stock so that the country may be safely piloted through hours of crisis and danger.

He then made an appeal for loyalty on the part of those who were henceforth to be his followers:

They (*i.e.* the Liberals) think that our loss may be their gain. Let us see that it is not. When a great figure is removed we learn, perhaps for the first time, how much we owe to him. The little murmurs, the small criticisms, which made his task more difficult, which added to the strain, the almost impossible strain, of those years of labour and anxiety – these things seem to us very small now. We think not of the minor and passing differences, but of the great underlying unity of purpose and of sympathy. Those murmurings and those criticisms did not matter very much so long as we had Mr. Bonar Law's great influence and his sure guidance to lead us through.

They would matter immensely now. And if I feel that I can undertake the charge which you entrust to me it is in the assurance that in the difficult days that lie ahead of us I shall have not merely your general support, but your generous forebearance in any mistakes that I may make, and that you yourselves as members of a great party will remember that you are a unity, that you too must stand together, not merely in support of your leaders but in support of one another. The load which we have to carry can only be carried successfully if we all work with a common purpose, if we all try to help one another, and each of us seeks to take his share in the difficult task that lies before us.

The Press as a whole was favourable, and Austen was re-assured to know "That the gibes and sneers of the last few years are not the real judgment of my countrymen upon me." The contrast between himself and his predecessor he well summed up in a letter at this time:

By the way it will amuse you as much as it did me to hear that when told the Party would certainly choose me the P.M. threw up his hands and cried, "he's an awful Tory", and that the Party appears to share the view that I am more of a Conservative than Bonar. And the odd thing is that it is true, for I have a tradition and he had none. I don't think that I ever heard him use an historic illustration or appeal to history or tradition or custom. The fact that he had no experience of government did not trouble him when he took the leadership. What he was afraid of then was his want of birth. He was confident that he could lead without experience, but afraid that the Party might follow unwillingly because he had not blue blood in his veins.

It's an odd world. How Lady Londonderry would have thrown herself on my neck if she had been still living ! I always used to say that the number of fingers she gave me – varying from 10 to 2 – was a sure sign of the state of my fortunes.

Nevertheless, in eighteen months the scene had changed again, and the Conservative Party once more took Bonar Law for its leader because it had by then come to consider him a better Tory than Austen. The Party meeting which took place at the Club on Thursday, October 19th, 1922, was the most famous ever held within the walls of the Carlton, and such being the case it will be as well to consider the circumstances in which it met.

The first nine months of 1922 had been marked by the growing unpopularity of the Coalition, and in consequence an increasing number of Conservatives wished to see their Party cut adrift from it for fear that they would otherwise go down with the sinking ship. The Government's unpopularity was further enhanced by its foreign policy, which seemed likely to lead to a needless war with Turkey, and at the beginning of September a letter reached Austen from Lord Derby to say that he could no longer support the Coalition on account of its policy in the Near East. Accordingly, a meeting of Ministers was held at Chequers on the 17th when there were present Lloyd George, Austen, Birkenhead, Churchill, Horne and Worthington-Evans. After much discussion it was decided to go to the country as a Coalition at the first favourable opportunity. Austen was, it may be added, not very sanguine of success, but the Prime Minister, Birkenhead, Horne, and Churchill were extremely optimistic. When this decision was communicated to Curzon and to Balfour, who was at Geneva when it was taken, they entirely agreed.

Thereafter events began to move rapidly. Austen proceeded to inform Sir George Younger, the chairman of the Party; Sir Malcolm Fraser, the Principal Agent; and Sir Leslie Wilson, the Chief Whip; of what had happened at Chequers, and of the intention of Ministers to go to the country as a Coalition Government. Younger replied that he was "frankly appalled"; Fraser feared there was "much trouble ahead, all round"; and Wilson was "very disturbed". To all this Austen replied that the discussions at Chequers had satisfied him that it was impossible to get rid of Lloyd George while retaining the support of his followers; but that if after the election the Prime Minister found himself with a mere fifty or sixty supporters of his own he would probably say that the new Parliament was not his, and would retire in favour of himself, Austen. This argument failed to convince either the chairman of the Party or the Chief Whip. All the same, on the 25th there was a meeting of the Conservative members of the Cabinet, and they all agreed with their leader except for Stanley Baldwin, who expressed his disapproval of what was proposed, but did not definitely refuse his assent.

External events were also assisting to precipitate a crisis. The Executive Committee of the National Union was due to meet on October 10th, and standing in the name of Miss Fardell was a motion that "the Executive Committee of the National Unionist Association desires to call the attention of the Leaders of the Party to the grave conditions of unrest in the Party, and to represent to them the necessity of bringing the Coalition to an end on friendly terms before the General Election which may be in the near future." True to his policy of hearing all points of view Austen asked Miss Fardell to come and see him, when he put to her the arguments which had convinced himself and his colleagues at Chequers, stressing especially the probability of extensive Socialist victories at the polls if the Coalition was dissolved before the general election took place. In deference to his request Miss Fardell consented to withdraw her motion, but Austen realized that this was only a danger averted.

Then there was an impending by-election at Newport. The seat had been held by a Coalition Liberal in 1918, and its tradition was Liberal. This time there were three candidates, namely, Lyndon Moore, a Liberal who described himself as being "without prefix or suffix"; J. W. Bowen, a Socialist; and Reginald, later Sir Reginald, Clarry, a Conservative. The Liberal was receiving the support of the Coalition Liberal organization in London, and the contest was generally regarded as a test case for the Coalition, more particularly as Clarry was being actively assisted by the dissident Conservatives, or Die-hards. The leaders of the Party did not believe that Clarry had any chance whatever of winning the seat, and they felt that the loss of Newport to the Socialists would lend considerable point to their argument in favour of continuing the Coalition.

There were almost daily meetings between the members of the Cabinet and the unofficial members of the Party in the hope of finding a way out of the difficulty, and at a dinner-party at Churchill's house on the 15th Austen offered a compromise in the shape of a meeting of the M.P.s at the Carlton. The next afternoon he met the Under-Secretaries[1], who were by this time in open revolt. Austen explained the decision which had been reached, but he did not succeed in appeasing the Junior Ministers to any appreciable extent. Nor, it may be added, did the course proposed recommend itself to the Executive Committee of the National Union, which considered that it, rather than the M.P.s, should be consulted.

On the morning of the 17th the Under-Secretaries, together with Baldwin, Griffith-Boscawen, and Younger, had a meeting with Leslie Wilson, when there was a long discussion as to the personal position of those present, and Baldwin and Griffith-Boscawen expressed themselves very strongly against serving under Lloyd George again. That afternoon Amery went to see Austen, and the two men had a long talk, though without the views of either being in any way modified in consequence. However, after he had left Austen it occurred to Amery that a compromise might be found on the basis of an election as things stood, but with the proviso

[1] There had been an earlier one on August 3rd.

that there should be a Party meeting after the election to consider the whole situation. Accordingly he secured, not without difficulty, the consent of the other Junior Ministers to this the next morning, and Wilson at once informed Austen of what had happened. Chamberlain was at first inclined to accept this compromise, and at lunch that day there was a general feeling in the Club that a settlement had been reached. However, on consulting his colleagues, in particular Birkenhead and Balfour, Austen found that they were opposed to Amery's suggestion, and he felt it to be his duty to stand by them.

As the 19th, the date fixed for the meeting at the Club, drew near it became increasingly obvious that everything depended upon the attitude which Bonar Law would adopt. He long remained undecided, and, indeed, he was so worried that he actually drafted a letter to his constituents resigning his seat in the House of Commons. In the late afternoon of the day preceding the meeting he saw Austen, and spoke with much sympathy for the latter's position. "He thought he would plead the state of his health and keep away from the meeting altogether, but in that case he must leave Parliament and give up public life. If he came to the meeting, he must speak against me," Austen wrote. "I told him that his speech would be decisive; the vote would go in his favour, the Government would have to resign, and he would have to form a new one." As Austen took his leave, Bonar Law said, "Well, it's a hateful position; I expect that if I had remained in your place I should have acted like you." After this interview Austen had no doubt of the attitude which Bonar Law would adopt at the meeting or of the result of the vote.

The morning of Thursday, October 19th, brought news which drove the final nail into the coffin of the Coalition, for contrary to all expectation Clarry was returned for Newport by a majority of over two thousand, with the Socialist second, and the Liberal a bad third. Of this result *The Times* said: "The country will see in it a most complete condemnation of the Coalition Government as such and a vindication of those Conservatives throughout the country who have been so determined to preserve their individuality in previous by-election contests." Furthermore, it was also announced that the Executive Committee of the National Unionist Association had unanimously passed a resolution to summon an emergency conference of the Party. The eyes of the whole country were fixed upon the Carlton Club.

The meeting had been called for eleven o'clock, and it was significant that at the very commencement the volume of cheering was very much greater for Bonar Law than it was for Austen Chamberlain. There were certainly no illusions on the part of Austen as to the attitude of the majority of those present, and he therefore made no effort to conciliate his opponents. He took the line that in the face of the growing Socialist strength co-operation with the Liberals was essential, and that though there would be a reconstruction of the Government after the election there must be no proscriptions in advance, for politics of exclusion and co-operation were incompatible. The existing Government would go to the country as a government, and it would be time to talk of changes when the victory had been won. These remarks were rather quietly received, and Baldwin met with a much warmer welcome for a short speech in which he said that he did not wish the dynamic force of the Prime Minister to break up the Conservative Party.

At this point Pretyman, who had, it will be remembered, proposed Austen's election as leader eighteen months before, moved a resolution to the effect that "this meeting of Conservative Members of the House of Commons declares its opinion that the Conservative Party, whilst willing to co-operate with the Coalition Liberals, should fight the election as an independent party with its own leader and its own programme". He was seconded by Colonel Lane-Fox. After one or two other speeches there were continued shouts for Bonar Law, who rose with obvious hesitation, and after a certain amount of soliloquizing made it clear that he thought the Party ought to come out of the Coalition, and go to the country with a mind to winning on its own. This statement evoked tremendous enthusiasm, and from that moment the issue was never really in doubt.

Balfour then rose, for Conservative peers who were members of the Government were present at the meeting though they had no right of voting, and proceeded to a philosophical analysis of the situation, finishing with the argument that no real difference of principle was at stake. The audience listened to this plea patiently, but gave no evidence whatsoever of being convinced.

When Balfour had finished Austen wished to put the motion to the vote, whereupon Leslie Wilson insisted upon speaking. Austen was extremely annoyed, but the Chief Whip felt that in the circumstances he could not remain silent. As he wrote many years later, "I tried to get Austen to change his views, and, having failed, I had no alternative but, as Chief Whip, knowing the facts and the views of over 180 Conservative Members of Parliament, to speak at the meeting." The line he took was to repeat strongly the arguments which Baldwin had used. Pretyman's motion was then put to the meeting, and carried by 187 votes to 87. Of the Ministers present only nine voted with Austen, while among the private members who supported him were Sir William Bull, Lieutenant-Commander (later Sir) Warden Chilcott, Walter Elliot, Thomas Inskip, and Kingsley Wood. Neville Chamberlain was on his way back from Canada when the meeting took place, and so was unable to vote. When the result was announced to Lloyd George he tendered his resignation to the King, who then called upon Bonar Law to form a government.

The reasons for the decisions taken at this meeting were admirably set out by Austen himself not long afterwards:

What was the result of the revolution finished at the Carlton Club? It is of course nonsense to describe it as a Belgravia intrigue or a revolt in the kitchen. It was first and foremost the matured result of eight years' rule by one Govt. which had to bear the blame not only for their mistakes but for all that went to make the general discontents; secondly of the Irish Treaty and of the consequent Die-hard movement which became formidable when it rallied round Salisbury and afforded an organization for the discontented; thirdly, of the growth of party feeling and party jealousy in the machine which is far too much run by old men and paid agents; lastly, the defects of Ll. G's character.

Such was the famous "Carlton Club Meeting" as it is generally called, and it is undoubtedly the best-known incident in the history of the Club.

CHAPTER VII

The Latest Age

THE First World War did not affect the West End Clubs so adversely as its successor was to do, but there were signs that had it lasted much longer some of them at any rate would have found themselves in a position of considerable difficulty. Indeed, in the early autumn of 1918 there was serious talk of amalgamation in certain circles. The younger members were serving overseas, and although London was very full of people, the people who filled it were not the people who used clubs. The subaltern back from the Somme or the Ypres Salient for a few days' leave was unlikely to spend it in the morning-room of his club even if he had one. The Armistice brought relief, for the return to normal conditions was much more rapid than was to be the case after the Second World War. A club here and there, the Isthmian was a notable example, was compelled to close its doors, but in the main the clubs resumed the even tenor of their pre-war way.

The Carlton was no exception. During the continuance of hostilities one breach with tradition had taken place, namely the employment of waitresses, who first made their appearance in the summer of 1915, but the girls proved so satisfactory that they remained after the Armistice. For the rest, the Club retained its prestige undimmed, and it was still a very important political centre. There can, too, be little doubt that its standing was further enhanced four years after the war by the famous meeting, described in the previous chapter, when the fate of a government was decided within its walls.

There was, nevertheless, one social revolution during the war years which by no means left the Club unaffected, and that was the growing tendency to entertain away from home. The Carlton has always had a large number of members living in the country, and many of them now found that they could no longer afford to run a London house; when they came to the capital it was either to stay in a flat or in a hotel. The pressure of taxation was also increasingly driving some town members to move into smaller quarters, while others moved out into the neighbouring countryside. On all hands, members were ceasing to entertain their friends at home, and were clamouring for a place to do so where the atmosphere should be more personal than in a hotel or restaurant.

The Carlton still shut its doors to all guests, and the slight air of mystery created by this policy was a definite asset. Nor was it a cause of much inconvenience before 1914 for the more sociable member had only to join some other club or clubs where visitors were permitted. After 1918 he was too often driven to a realization of the fact that he could no longer afford several clubs, and so the question arose of what the Carlton could do to meet his requirements.

In 1925, No. 7 Carlton Gardens was purchased from the Earl of Dudley, and became the Carlton Club Annexe. This not only enabled members to entertain guests, but it also afforded bedroom accommodation. All this was made financially possible by the issue of Bonds to the amount of £60,000 which were taken up by members, the final repayment being in 1941, and at the same time the standard rate of subscription was raised to seventeen guineas: the prices charged in the new building were also slightly higher than those obtaining in the Club itself. The annexe immediately obtained widespread support among the members, and during the fifteen years of its existence it was one of the most important social centres of London. Both the cooking and the service were of the very best, and invitations to lunch or dine at 7 Carlton Gardens were eagerly accepted. Evening-dress was compulsory, and thereby hangs a tale. One night in September the then Prime Minister, Stanley Baldwin, and his wife entered the annexe in day clothes, and sat down to dinner. The steward, Bartlett, came over to them, and called their attention to the rule, whereupon Baldwin went to every occupied table in the room, and apologized for his unorthodox attire, excusing himself on the ground that 10 Downing Street was closed and that he was himself only passing through London.

On another occasion the future King Paul of the Hellenes lunched at the annexe with some friends, and when he was leaving the hall porter, Learner, was somewhat puzzled by the fact that there did not appear to be any royal hat. The explanation proved to be that the Crown Prince, as he then was, possessed a limitless amount of headgear for his various uniforms, but had no ordinary hat to wear with a lounge suit.

The end came with the bombing of the Club itself on October 14th, 1940. The annexe was not directly hit by H.E. bombs it is true, but it was extensively damaged by incendiaries. At various times suggestions were put forward that it might be used as temporary premises by the Club, or re-opened as the annexe, but they proved impracticable, chiefly because the building had no separate kitchens. So closed another, and extremely happy, chapter in the Club's history.

The old tradition of admitting female guests only into the Club on special occasions, which had existed since 1837, was maintained, but apart from the Coronation of King George VI and Queen Elizabeth in 1937 it was confined to the nights of a general election. After the First World War such evenings acquired an added interest since the polling now took place everywhere on the same day, and the scene in the Club was particularly animated as the results came pouring in: especially was this the case on the night of the general election of 1931 when the Conservative Party won the most resounding victory in its history, and its leader, Stanley Baldwin, appeared in the Club in the middle of the rejoicings.

In 1935 an incident occurred which throws an interesting light upon the wide reactions of the international tension existing at that date. There was still no regulation to the effect that candidates for election must be British subjects, and in that year Brigadier-General Wade Hayes, an American citizen, was elected a member. Soon afterwards it became known that a retired Bulgarian diplomat of unimpeachable respectability was about to be put forward by his son-in-law, a Scottish baronet. This news was not long in reaching the German embassy, and information came to the then chairman, Lord Clanwilliam, to the effect that if the Bulgarian was elected then two or three members of the embassy staff, to whom no objection could be taken on the score of birth or political opinions, would at once be put forward for election. This would have destroyed the whole character of the Club, and Ministers, far from being able to relax in conversation with their friends, would have had to have been continually on their guard in case their remarks were overheard by the representatives of some foreign, and possibly none too friendly, power. The committee was not slow to appreciate what was at stake, and so the existing rule came into effect that the proposer and seconder must "vouch that the Candidate is a British Subject".

So the years between the two wars passed by without any notable event in the Club's history save for the opening of the annexe, and the tragic death in 1931 of the secretary, Brigadier-General Baird, in a motoring accident. At the same time it would be idle to deny that the Club declined as a political force during the period. No further Party meetings took place within its walls, and the Conservative leaders did not use it so much as in the past, indeed the time soon came when some of them were not even members. The back benchers not unnaturally arrived at the conclusion that they might as well follow the example which had been set them, more particularly as it affected their pockets very favourably; and in these circumstances there was no great inducement for the young man with political aspirations to get his name put down in the candidates' book. What may without exaggeration be described as the drift away from active politics was accentuated when Arthur's closed its doors, and a good many of its members were absorbed by the Carlton in April 1940: they were, of course, Conservatives, but they were not particularly interested in politics as such. At this point it may not, perhaps, be out of place to contradict the oft-quoted statement that any and every Conservative peer and M.P. has an automatic right of election to the Carlton. This is not the case: such persons, together with the heirs apparent to peerages, certainly enjoy priority, but they have to come up for election by the committee like any other candidate.

It has been well said that the history of the West End clubs is the history of London manners since the Restoration, and, as we have seen, the changes in taste, habits, and customs of the nineteenth century were plainly reflected in the life of the Carlton; nor was that period which has been so well termed the Twenty Years' Armistice any exception. The manners and customs of members changed as those of the outside world were changing. At the end of the First World War it was not unknown to see members sitting about the club-house in their hats, and Lord Clanwilliam kept up the custom until his death in 1953. The twenty-sixth Earl of Crawford, who died in 1913, is said to have been the last member to have a meal in the coffee-room in a top-hat, but there were a good many other taboos which continued to exist until the twenties of the present century. The new member was, for example, warned that he would be well-advised not to sit in the window of the smoking-room until he had been elected for at least two years, and he must eschew the tables near the fire in the coffee-room until he was a Privy Councillor or at least an Under-Secretary. On the other hand, to sit at one of the tables along the wall was a confession of failure: they were called Brook Street, "because no one knew the people who lived there".

In another place[1] the present author has described his experiences on being first elected to the Carlton, and as these were typical, not exceptional, they may, perhaps, be quoted here:

One of the most frightening experiences in ordinary life is the first visit to a club of which one has just been elected a member. The apologetic explanation of who you are to the Hall Porter; the haunting fear that you have unwittingly taken the chair of the outstanding figure of the club, some man renowned all over the

[1] *Chapters of Life*, pp. 198–99.

world for his exploits in peace and war; and, above all, the suspicion that by your behaviour you are confirming the servants in their belief that the type of member now being elected is very different from what used to be the case: all these are emotions which no clubman is ever likely to forget.

I have experienced them on several occasions, but never more strongly than when I was elected to the Carlton in 1921 at the age of twenty-five, its youngest member at that time.[1] Walter Long had proposed me, and he very kindly introduced me to the club himself, although he was by no means well and had, in fact, recently been compelled to relinquish the office of First Lord of the Admiralty owing to ill-health. The Carlton in those days was a much more formidable institution than it has since become, and as visitors were not admitted the new Member had no idea what he would find when he first crossed the threshold. In my case all went well under Long's chaperonage, and in any event we went to the club about noon on a spring morning when it was practically empty. I was told where, as a new Member, I should and should not sit, and I was warned that if I wanted to wear a hat in the Club it must be a silk one. I was then given a glass of the most excellent sherry, accompanied by a warning against cocktails to which I was informed Eric[2] was unfortunately partial in preference to superior beverages. Long then took his departure, and I felt particularly forlorn: soon the Club began to fill up with Members coming in for lunch, and I slunk away.

My real agony took place some weeks later when, one particularly hot night of that very hot summer, I mustered up courage to go to the Carlton again, and to dine there. I put on a dinner-jacket, and I tried to remember all the instructions which I had been given. I drank one glass of sherry, as I felt that a second might give an impression of a partiality for the bottle unbecoming in a young man; I took care to read a paper of which there were several copies lying on the table in the morning-room in case I should be accused of monopolizing the one which my elders and

---

[1] Brigadier Sir Alexander Stanier, Bt., questions this, and asserts his own claim to the distinction.
[2] The present (third) Viscount Long of Wraxall.

betters might want to peruse; and I ordered my dinner for an hour which I trusted would not be considered too early or too late. On entering the coffee-room I chose a table which seemed to be neither too conspicuous nor too inconspicuous, and having seated myself I felt things had not gone too badly.

At the next table to mine there was an elderly Member reading the evening paper. Half-way through dinner he suddenly said, "Do you think this fine weather is going to continue?" I was so startled at being spoken to in such early days of my Membership that I could only stammer out a few words in reply to the question. Whereupon my neighbour endeavoured to put me at my ease. "I see," he said, "you are astonished at me speaking to you since you are a new Member. Well, you'll find a lot of narrow-minded fellows in this club, but I'm very broad-minded myself: I hold the view that if a man is fit to be elected to the Club, he is fit to be spoken to when he gets inside it." Several months elapsed, and the fogs of November had shrouded Pall Mall in darkness, before I again ventured into the Carlton Club.

That was a long time ago, and the Carlton soon came to be one of the friendliest clubs in London; indeed, it would have been unrecognizable by those who derived their impressions of it from Low's cartoons in the *Evening Standard* or from the slighting references in the Radical and Socialist Press. What greatly attributed to the comfort of the Club during these years was the excellence of the staff, and in this connection three men in particular stand out, namely Bonner, the hall porter, and Bartlett and Learner, respectively steward and hall porter in the annexe. The members of those days owed these three a great debt of gratitude, which was freely and frankly acknowledged on all sides.

Of course the members were not equal in point of charm, and one or two were a definite nuisance to their fellows. Not long before the Second World War a certain noble earl, largely owing to a weakness for the bottle which he had acquired in middle life, was in very straightened financial circumstances, and was reduced so low that he used to borrow five shillings at one end of the smoking-room and then spend it on whisky at the other. Each year his fellow-members hoped that he would have to resign owing to inability to pay his subscription, for he had become a definite liability to the Club, but each year some old friend of his father, who had been a very great man in his day, came to his rescue. Finally, he was on the verge of bankruptcy, when he was saved by a collection being made for the appeasement of his creditors. Unhappily, the sum subscribed was about twelve hundred pounds in excess of what was required, and it was made over to him more or less on the understanding that he left the country. This proved to be the complete undoing of him, for he departed to France, where he died in the depths of degradation during the German occupation of that country.

An equal nuisance, if for a shorter time, to the members was another peer, also an earl. When sober he could be a very charming fellow, but once he had drink inside him he became truculent and violent. He had, in the end, to resign for having struck a fellow-member down with a chair in the hall, and his subsequent career proved that the Carlton was definitely the gainer by his resignation. He was also a member of the Thames Yacht Club, and one evening there after he had been drinking heavily he was descending the staircase when he encountered a new member in the process of ascending it, The second man made every endeavour to avoid his lordship, and the staircase is a broad one; but the peer was swaying from side to side to such an extent that this proved impossible, and a collision took place. On this his lordship enquired roughly whether the other man knew who he was. The reply came to the effect that the man who was ascending the stairs

was a new member; that it was the first time he had been in
the club since his election; and that he knew no one there
except his proposer and seconder. "Then see you b——y well
remember me the next time we meet", bellowed the nobleman, and hit the second man under the jaw with such force
that he went down the whole flight of stairs. The inevitable
happened; his lordship had to resign from the Thames Yacht
Club as he had done from the Carlton; and he died some years
afterwards without a club at all.

The Club also had its eccentrics, and the exploits of one of
them became the talk of the West End. The member in
question was quite harmless, and his behaviour can be estimated by one notable incident. He had a rooted aversion to
leaving the Club when it closed at night, and this usually
necessitated a search for him by the night porter and such
other servants as were available. On one occasion he eluded
his pursuers, but in the early hours of the morning a light was
observed in the gallery which ran round the hall. On investigation the member in question was found lying on the floor
reading an evening-paper by the light of a number of
sealing-wax candles which he had taken from the writing-
tables and had arranged around him in a sort of fairy circle.

No account of the Club's activities at this time could pretend
to be complete which did not contain at any rate a mention
of The Honourable Company of the Round Table, which
was a club in the Club. It started in or about the month of
January, 1917, with a few members who used to lunch
regularly at a round table in the coffee-room, and in due
course they formed themselves into a small society which
from time to time held a dinner. Major Field-Richards, who
was one of its most prominent members, writes: "It never had
a constitution, but a Candidate when suggested by a Member

was brought to lunch; if approved, he was invited a second time, and if confirmed was told that he would be included among the Members. Politically it had no functions or aspirations. A *sine qua non* was to be (i) a decent fellow, (ii) with no axe to grind, and (iii) one who was always willing to advise a fellow-member in any difficulty where his experience and knowledge would be of help. At the Dinners we usually sat down about 37-44 at a price all included of never more than £2 2s. od. and usually about 38s. The Table died when we were blitzed." To some extent the place of The Honourable Company of the Round Table was filled by the formation, a few years after the Second World War, of the O.B.s[1], who dine together on the first Tuesday in every month, except August and September.

The coming of the Second World War not unnaturally affected the Club in exactly the same way as it did the rest of the country. At first there was general apprehension of large-scale air attack, but then as the weeks went by and nothing of the sort took place life returned to something approaching normal, save for the inconvenience of the blackout. With the German attack on France and the Low Countries, and the fall of the Chamberlain administration in May, 1940, the scene changed again, and the Club reflected the tension which was being felt all over the country. During May and June both it and the annexe were very crowded, as London was full of people up on public or private business, but when the threat of invasion appeared more imminent many of them departed to do what might be required of them elsewhere. Such was the course of events leading up to the tragic night of October 14th, 1940.

What happened then is best described in a letter written

[1] The exact significance of these letters has never been authoritatively stated.

on the following day by Sir Clive Morrison-Bell, Bt., to the chairman:

October 15th, 1940

My dear Clanwilliam,

I rather think you had left the Carlton last night before this tragedy, and so I feel you may be interested to hear some further details of the actual occurrence; perhaps some of the Members, too, who are out of town might like to hear something of the end of the stout-hearted old Club, which we have all, over a period of years, come to love.

In a sense I am in a good position to tell the story, for though there were some ten or more Members sitting together talking in the centre of the morning-room, I was musing myself in the far corner of the room to the right of the door as you go in; having just put down the evening-paper, I was sitting there looking for a moment towards the Pall Mall end of the room, and thinking it was about time to go and have some dinner. In what immediately followed I somehow seemed to feel myself a kind of fascinated spectator in the back row of the stalls, taking an objective sort of interest in the unbelievable and amazing goings-on at the far end of the room. I suppose really before darkness supervened it could only have been a matter of a few seconds, perhaps ten or twelve at the outside, and yet what happened all seemed to me at the time, for some unexplained reason, to be following quite an orderly course. I tried during what proved to be rather a sleepless night to reconstruct what must have more or less taken place.

It would be just about 8.30 P.M. For some moments a 'plane seemed to have been hovering about somewhere overhead, when suddenly one instinctively realized the final rushing sound of an approaching bomb. Immediately came the most appalling and frightful crash. I will not attempt to describe it, for by now most Members will have a pretty good idea of the deafening noise that a nearby bomb makes; but I think it would take the Prime Minister himself adequately to paint the effect of a high explosive bomb at what might be described as the far end of the room. I heard Colonel Willis[1] say next morning that he thought there were two

---

[1] The Secretary.

bombs, and I am inclined to agree that he is right in this, for I remember quite distinctly a sort of double sequence. First appeared from near the far fire-place a great triangular wedge of brick, something which might be described as looking like a large slice of brown cake. It appeared, from where I sat, as if it might be the fire-place wall being forced out by the explosion across the room in an easterly direction; then immediately afterwards, in reality I dare say not much more than a split second, another large brown slice came crashing down. This, in a way, seems rather to confirm the theory of a second and almost simultaneous bomb. If, as it appeared likely, it was the fire-place wall coming out into the morning-room, this would immediately let loose the ceiling and with it the library floor, and so on right up to the roof itself. So down this brown avalanche crashed on to what used to be the newspaper table. It was rather like thunder rolling down, and with just at first the slightest break, which might or might not fit in with the second bomb theory. In fact I seemed to have time to take in a sort of wave of crashes approaching the centre of the room towards where the little group of Members were sitting. Then something new occurred. Great masses of black smoke came pouring through the swing-doors from the hall across the room, blown no doubt by the explosion but obviously not the explosion itself, for nobody in the direct path, as these ten Members would have been, could have survived.

One might here pause to ask where did the actual explosion force go? Across the room at the far end I should think, and fortunately not up it, or surely by the blast we should all have been blown to smithereens. Besides a lot of it must evidently have been taken up and absorbed by the stoutness of the building itself and the solidity of its walls. My theory, for what it is worth – and an inspection of the building might alter it in many aspects – is that the bomb (or bombs) came through somewhere about the corner of the committee room, perhaps not far from where the old wireless used to stand; then some of the wall went out, letting down the roof, but with the other wall (that cross wall near the fireplace) holding, so that the force was thus diverted across instead of up the room. It is a chastening thought to reflect that had all this occurred about twenty minutes later, it would almost certainly have found most, if not all, of the Members gathered around the wireless in the Library upstairs to hear the nine o'clock news, and they would thus have been not very far away from the direct path of the bomb.

But to return to the story; the danger still seemed to be the roof. It was crashing down in tons. What was going to stop the advance? "Look out, there", I instinctively shouted, though in that din could hardly have been heard, and anyhow what could any of them have done? And then came darkness, thick darkness with choking black smoke and a bitter acrid taste that dried up one's throat.

All this takes some time to describe, I know, but it could really have been only a matter of a few seconds. And what stopped the roof coming down until the whole thing was on our heads? I really don't know, but I should have liked to have had a look inside, by daylight, to have seen if there was some structural reason. Anyhow I now found myself wondering – for the objective spectator attitude had faded and in a flash given place to the personal-safety factor – will this roof-crashing reach *my* corner, and, at the best, bottle me up where I am sitting? It is an extraordinary circumstance that the roof with its many tons of girders and masonry must have stopped coming down within a few feet of where the Members were sitting; I rather think it was Victor Warrender who was sitting in the circle with his back to the window, and this mass of rubble must have come down within four or five feet of his chair, and anyhow it was only a foot or two more from the others; the high tide probably reached up to that red-leather sofa that faced the Pall Mall windows.

There now seemed to be a sort of horrified pause of a second or two, and then I suppose we all sprang to our feet. Through the din, I could hear far-away voices – "Are you there; is anybody hurt there; here give me your hand; who is this, are you sure there is nobody hurt," for it must be remembered that we now seemed to be enveloped in inky darkness. Somebody said, "Better try and get to the door," and it was then that I moved across to join up. In this little groping party I cannot recall all who were there, but I remember the Chief Whip (Margesson),

Shakespeare Morrison, Harold Macmillan, Ramsbotham, Cross, Lord Hailsham, and evidently young Hogg, for I could hear the latter saying, "It is quite alright, Father, it is quite alright", and I think Lord Hailsham replying, "Yes, I am sure it is." There were one or two more whom I could not see in the dark; it might interest you to find out who the others were. I flashed a small torch I happened to have in my pocket, but it was hardly possible to see one's hand with it, owing to the thick and smelly clouds of black smoke.

But after all was it, as Lord Hailsham said alright? How much more roof was coming down? What kept it up now? Was there still a floor to cross on or had that gone too? And so slowly towards the door, and out into the hall, the little party moved, now all close together. What about that gallery? Has it come down, or is it going to? What about the stairs, are they still there? The feeble light hardly showed anything, but the stairs were as a matter of fact still there, even if the balustrading had gone, and slowly the little group felt its way down towards the front door. Somebody said, "Where is Willis? Can we do anything to help him?" And another voice, "He has probably gone down below to find out about his staff." At the foot of the stairs a large heavy door was on the floor, and had to be picked up and laid on one side before the street was finally reached, where the first thing to be seen were about twenty incendiary bombs spluttering away all round. I saw somebody, I think it was the Hall Porter, go up and kick one; it barked at him, and exploded, and he kicked it again and shortly got it out. Apparently a Molotov breadbasket had been released with the bombs. The appalling extent of the damage could only be fully realized next morning, when great blocks were lying about in the street, some of which must have weighed about a ton. In fact as I was moving that night along the pavement, or rather climbing over the debris, I suddenly heard a heavy thud just a few feet behind me, in fact unpleasantly close. It must have been a dilatory block that had decided to come down, and the following morning I noticed a lump there about the size of a small suit-case that from its position fitted in with my particular thud.

Looking back, perhaps the most wonderful thing about it all was that everybody, both the Members and the Staff, seems to have got away from that inferno without a scratch; strange, nay providential, when it can with truth be said that death itself was stalking through the Club.

Well, Mr. Chairman, you have lost a beautiful historic and very lovely Club, and both you and your Committee will have the warmest and deepest sympathy from all your Members.

The stout old walls are still standing there, or at least they were this morning. They stood up to the fearful tearing and rending of Goering's high explosive bombs, and let us hope that this may be symbolic of the best elements of Conservatism down the ages to come.

Yours very sincerely,
Clive Morrison-Bell.

The immediate problem of where the members should go was temporarily solved by the generous and spontaneous offers of hospitality which at once came in from the other West End clubs. Such an attitude was the more commendable as both food and drink were, as the saying went in those wartime days, "in short supply", and no club relished the prospect of sharing its meagre store of either with the members of another.

The question of the ultimate future was far more difficult. The most cursory examination showed that the restoration of the Club and the annexe would be a very expensive business, and certainly could not be carried out while the war lasted, nor in all probability for several years after it had finished. Fortunately, Arthur's old premises at 69 St. James's Street, the original home of White's, were still empty, and so the Carlton was enabled to establish itself there. As that is still its home, and is likely to be for many a long year to come, some account of Arthur's may not be out of place in a history of the Carlton.

It owed its designation to one Robert Arthur who for some years owned White's, and was the son of that John Arthur who had been assistant to Francis White, the original proprietor of White's Chocolate House. "When Francis White died in 1711," writes Brigadier-General C. G. Higgins in the *Field*, "his wife Elizabeth assumed the management and retained it until about 1730, when she handed it over to John Arthur. According to the rate book, John Arthur appears from the year 1702 to have been the occupant of 69 St. James's Street, so it would seem that Francis White must have sub-let the premises to him from that date, possibly without vesting him with the management of the Chocolate House. John Arthur died in 1734, and was succeeded by his son Robert, who is shown in the rate book as the occupier of 69 St. James's Street from 1734 to 1756. Various books of reference have stated that Arthur's Club was founded in 1765, that was the year after Robert Arthur's death, but as far as the managers of the club were aware, no mention of Arthur's can be found from the time of Robert Arthur's death until the year 1811 – and this year must therefore be accepted as the date of the club's foundation. This was nearly fifty years after Arthur had died; none of the original members of Arthur's Club, founded in 1811, could have known him, and it would, therefore, seem that the only reason the club was named after him was owing to the fact that he had once rented the house they proposed to take for their club house."

Arthur's was never a cheap club, and the original subscription was twenty guineas. Frank Wallace, in *Happier Years*, remarks that in its later years the food "was rather more expensive than in some other clubs". At one time, too, a good deal of gambling went on there, though the members never acquired quite the reputation of those of White's and

Brooks's in that respect, and we are told that in 1836 "a nobleman of the highest reputation and influence in society was detected at Arthur's cheating at cards, and after a trial which did not go in his favour, died of a broken heart".

No mention of Arthur's, however brief, would be complete without at least an allusion to Kitty Fischer, of whom an engraving used to hang in the hall, but which is now to be seen in the committee room of Pratt's; for it was bought by the late Duke of Devonshire after Arthur's closed its doors. The lady in question was the daughter of a German stay-maker, and at an early age she became one of the leading *demimondaines* of the day, or, to put it less brutally, "her companionship was eagerly sought by many men of wealth and fashion". There was a tradition in Arthur's that Kitty Fischer was for some time kept by subscription of the whole club, but unfortunately for romance the relevant dates do not tally with this attractive legend. Kitty died in 1767 "a victim of cosmetics", and, as we have seen, Arthur's was not founded until 1811. There was, however, an establishment called the Miles Club at 69 St. James's Street between the removal of White's and the foundation of Arthur's, so it may have been the members of this club who jointly subscribed for the enjoyment of Kitty's favours.

To quote Frank Wallace again: "The members of Arthur's were the most part country gentlemen of a type which has done much for our land in the past. They took their duties seriously, and upheld the traditions of country life which it is to be hoped, in spite of changes and vicissitudes, their successors will be able to imitate. The outlook on life of some may have been narrow, but no one could deny that the majority lived up to their code. I once took a German to lunch there. It was an unfortunate day, for looking round the dining-room he whispered, 'Tell me, do all the members have to be over sixty before they are admitted?' His parting remark was more encouraging. Said he, 'Now I know what English gentlemen are like. That is what we want to be – a nation of *Herrenvolk*.' It seems likely that a considerable period will elaspse before such an ambition is realized."

Like all clubs worth the name Arthur's did not take kindly to new ideas. "It must have been", Frank Wallace records, "I fancy, about the year 1922 that an automatic lift was installed. Shortly afterwards, one Sunday morning, a trio of adventurous veterans decided to inspect the innovation. Pressing accordingly the button which set the affair in motion, they started on their Odyssey. At the outset all went according to plan. Suddenly, for reasons unknown, between two floors they came to a dead stop. It was, as I have said, the Seventh Day[1]. At such times the comings and goings, part of normal club life, are to a great extent stilled. The preliminary outburst of the trio, designed with a view to procuring outside assistance, swelled by degrees to baffled bellowings only comparable to those of a wounded buffalo. Gradually their volume dwindled, and finally, save for an occasional muffled groan, died away. I forget the period of their incarceration, but when rescued they were nearly asphyxiated as there was no ventilation. 'Serve 'em damned well right', growled one old diehard as the news spread, 'for shoving in such newfangled contraptions'."

Such were the traditions of the club into whose premises the Carlton now moved, and it will be for the historian of the future to decide whether the members were thereafter the more affected by club heredity or by club environment.

---

[1] With great respect to Frank Wallace, Sunday is the first, not the seventh day of the week.

It has already been suggested that the admission of a number of the former members of Arthur's may have tended to create a less actively political atmosphere in the Carlton, and their return to their old home undoubtedly revived a good many of their old traditions which would otherwise in all probability have died. At the same time, 69 St. James's Street has never been to the Carlton veterans quite like their old quarters, and comfortable as it is they find it on occasion impossible to repress feelings of nostalgia. Today a new generation of members and servants is growing up who never knew Pall Mall, and they have recently received a considerable reinforcement from those who belonged to the now defunct Marlborough-Windham, so the memory of the old Carlton is gradually being effaced.

Of one thing there can be no question, and that is regarding the architectural merit of the new premises. "The clubhouse", says an article in *Country Life*, "is among the most interesting and least altered of those which arose in such numbers during the early years of the nineteenth century – that golden age of the London club. Arthur's dignified *façade* is one of those which still impart a classic flavour to St. James's Street even after all that the changes of recent years have done to impair its architectural character." The outstanding feature of the interior is the main staircase, dividing into two, surmounted by a cupola-shaped and domed window. The ceilings, it will be generally agreed, are fine; the rooms lofty and well proportioned; and all the doors are of fine mahogany. Indeed, it has been said that "a general aspect of calm and dignity pervades the whole house". Of the old Carlton, on the other hand, it is recorded that an irreverent new member once declared that it was like a duke's house, with the duke lying dead upstairs.

The decision to house the Carlton permanently at 69 St. James's Street was not taken until many other possibilities had been examined, including a return to the old premises in Pall Mall. There is no point in discussing the alternatives here, but there is every reason to suppose that the final decision was the right one. With the whole future of West End clubs so obscure it would have been too great a risk to rebuild on the scale of the plans which were drawn up, even if the money had been available, and the subscription would probably have had to be raised to a figure far beyond the pockets of those who would be called upon to pay it. Nothing today is on the magnificent scale that existed in the past, and the Carlton could hardly expect to prove an exception.

A number of amenities had to be sacrificed, and among them was the Library, which had been one of the glories of the old Club. After the bombing it was housed at Canonbury, on the suggestion of Mr. John Watson and by courtesy of the Marquess of Northampton. When it became clear that there would be no return to Pall Mall a good many of the books were sold, and others put in store, for only a very small selection could be housed in 69 St. James's Street. The fact has had to be faced in connection with the books as with much else that the Carlton may well in the future have to be run upon less ambitious lines.

EPILOGUE

URING the course of the foregoing narrative there have been many illustrations of the way in which changing social and political conditions have affected the life of the Carlton Club since its foundation a century and a half ago: in some ways the Carlton has probably been more affected by these changes than many other similar institutions, and at the risk of a certain amount of repetition it may not be without value or interest to assess them in the light of the past, but also with an eye to the future.

In the first place it must never be forgotten that the Carlton is not only a social club, but also a political one, and the foremost political club in the world. Comparisons with the Knickerbocker Club in New York, though often made, are thus beside the point. In consequence, it is, and always has been, peculiarly susceptible to changes both of a social and of a political nature. When it was founded, and throughout the earlier years of its existence, the Conservative Party, both in and out of Parliament, was firmly based on those classes of the community, namely the upper and upper-middle, which normally and naturally aspired to membership of such an institution. There were, it is true, individuals of somewhat different origin – Disraeli was himself a notable instance – who stormed the ramparts of privilege, but once they had proved their worth they were admitted on equal terms, and they soon settled down in their new surroundings.

Nothing is more remarkable than the difference between Whig and Tory practice in this respect. The great Whig magnates never trusted men like Burke and Sheridan as other than *parvenus* who were extremely useful, and even in the later years of the nineteenth century the same feelings influenced the relations between Gladstone and Joseph

Chamberlain: as Julian Amery has so well put it, "Gladstone persistently underestimated the Birmingham manufacturer and his hold over the British democracy. When concessions had to be made, he seldom concealed his reluctance in yielding. Nor did he ever encourage those private contacts which alone might have led to better understanding. In the event, his failure to conciliate Chamberlain wrecked both his party and his policy."[1]

All this was in marked contrast with the conditions obtaining in the Tory camp, where very different treatment was meted out to Canning, Huskisson, and Peel: nor has the precedent been broken down to our own time, though it would clearly be invidious to mention living examples of its application. Such being the case it is not too much to say that for many decades the Carlton Club served as the depot where the new recruits to the Conservative Party learned their drill. There never was – nor is there today – any snobbery in the Club itself: whatever a man's origin, once he has been elected a member he is regarded and treated as an equal by his fellow-members. On an earlier page we have seen how anxious Disraeli, who had little in common with the average Tory when he first entered public life, was to become a member of the Carlton, and how happy he was once he had been elected. In this way the Club may be said to have been the microcosm of the Conservative Party, and the perpetuation of this tradition in the vastly changed circumstances of today is one of the more urgent problems facing it at the present time.

One reason why the Carlton was able for so long to combine the *rôles* of rallying-point and melting-pot was that its members used it as a club and not merely as a restaurant. They came together there to discuss the problems of the day, and after any big event at Westminster the leaders of the Conservative Party went there to hear the views of their followers. Of late years, and particularly since the Second World War, this state of affairs has, as we have seen, tended to pass away; the M.P. of today has perforce to spend most

[1] *The Life of Joseph Chamberlain,* vol. IV., p. 455

of his life either at the House of Commons or in his constituency, and he has little leisure, even if he possesses the
inclination, to converse with his fellow-men in the Carlton
Club. What is true of the rank-and-file applies with even
greater force to the leaders of the party, the call upon whose
time is infinitely greater than it was even a generation ago.
As for the old habit of looking in at the Club on the way
home for a drink after the House has risen this is no longer
feasible when the average M.P., far from living in the West
End as in the past, probably resides at least as far away as
Hampstead or Kensington, and wishes to get back there as
soon as possible. This development is to be regretted on every
score, for it means that the politicians are being increasingly
segregated and kept away from any but other politicians, and
in the case of the Carlton it is depriving the Club of one of
the main spheres of its usefulness and interest, not least for the
younger men entering public life.

In fact the internal combustion engine has brought about
a greater social revolution than has ever been effected by the
doctrines of Rousseau or Marx, and the present generation is
removed by centuries from the age when the committee of
the Carlton found it most convenient to meet on a Saturday
afternoon. Seventy years ago a member was either in the
country or in London: if he was in the country he did not use
the Club; if he was in London he probably spent a large
portion of his time there. Today he probably lives anything
up to forty miles out of London, and comes up to his office on
five days of the week, for the country gentlemen whose
interests are primarily rural is rare these days. When he is in
London he may well have his lunch at the Carlton, but he
does not sit over it, and he is not often to be found there in
the evening because he only stays up in town as the result of
some special engagement, whether of a business or social
nature. At the weekend for a variety of reasons which do not
concern us here, he is not in London at all.

With the growth of big cities in the middle of last century
and particularly of London, men who had to live in them

started going to clubs because there was nowhere else that they could conveniently go in view of the fact that their movements were circumscribed by the lack of the necessary transport: now that their movements are not so circumscribed the clubs are suffering. Of course this consideration applies to all clubs, both social and political, but for a political club like the Carlton the threat is a double one, for if it is not used socially then its political importance and prestige will inevitably suffer.

Another factor which has done a great deal to modify the old traditions of club life as it was lived in Victorian and Edwardian times has been the change in the position of women in just that section of the community from which clubmen are drawn. The days are gone when a man went down to his club for a few hours while his wife remained at home engaged in either looking after the children or servants, or in sewing a fine seam. Children and servants are now in short supply, while husbands and wives tend to go about more together, and these developments have adversely affected the clubs. To some extent the challenge has been met either by the institution of a women's annexe, or even by throwing the clubs open to women guests; but this does not really touch the root of the trouble, which is that on holidays or at weekends members and their wives have formed the habit of going out of London altogether in their cars.

Above all, there is the question of finance which calls for attention, and that under two heads, namely the monetary resources of the members, which have steadily diminished, and the cost of running a club, which has as steadily increased. Broadly speaking, the class from which members of West End clubs are drawn has been the most hardly hit by the World Wars of this century, and by the rampant inflation which has followed the second of them. It is true that there is a small minority of businessmen who have their subscriptions paid for them by their firms, but they represent an inconsiderable proportion of the total membership. At the turn of the century it is safe to say that the vast majority of the members of the Carlton were men whose incomes were wholly or largely indirect, but that class has virtually ceased to exist. The Carlton was, like Arthur's, never a poor man's club, but today there are very many members who can barely afford the subscription, and who have to look very carefully indeed at every penny they spend within its walls: particularly does this apply to the younger married men in the professions.

Some club committees have gone out of their way to meet this demand by the provision of swimming baths, cocktail bars, and squash courts, but it is at least doubtful whether they have solved the problem, for many of the younger men, paradoxically enough, seem to hanker after membership of clubs where these amenities do not exist. Even had it been willing the Carlton would not have been able to indulge in these luxuries for in its present premises the space is lacking. In any event there is the rivalry of Hurlingham to be taken into account. At Hurlingham every kind of sporting facility is provided, and of its 2,500 members not a few do not belong to any other club, while it is now increasingly used during the winter months for social purposes so that as a competitor to the West End clubs it cannot be ignored.

Lastly, before the First World War it was by no means uncommon for a man to have two clubs, one purely social in its composition, and the other associated with the Services, the Universities, or a particular political party. This is still the ideal, but the number of those who have the means to attain it is rapidly decreasing. Reliable evidence is lacking as to the choice which in these circumstances is being made, but the lesson for the Carlton would seem to be that if it is to continue to attract it will have to do so largely on account of political prestige.

Then there is the second financial consideration, namely the ever-increasing cost of running a club: not only does this militate against the provision of fresh amenities, but it has also made difficult the maintenance of existing ones, with unfortunate effects upon membership. It is not, as is sometimes alleged, that the clubs were bad employers in the past, for the wages quoted on earlier pages as paid by the Carlton were normal for the period: what has happened has been that owing largely to inflation the internal purchasing power of the pound has gone down, but whereas wages have been raised until they more than compensate their recipients for this fall, the income of the average club member is very far indeed from having risen correspondingly. Nor has there been a corresponding rise in the rate of the subscription: taking the purchasing power of the pound as twenty shillings in July, 1914, it was 12s. 5d. (62p) in July, 1939, and 2s. 9d. (13.7p) today, whereas the subscription to the Carlton was fifteen guineas in 1914 and it is £55 today. From these figures it is possible to argue that it should have been raised more steadily and more steeply over the period.

At the same time no one can accuse the committee during the past ten or fifteen years of not facing up to these difficulties, and in the effort to overcome them the most revolutionary changes have taken place – indeed some of the older members have been heard to declare that it is no longer a club at all but a restaurant. A bar has been instituted, to which male guests are admitted, and there are no rooms to which visitors may not be taken save the smoking-room, while even there exceptions are permitted in the case of the young. Most recently a supper-room has been opened in the basement, on the analogy of Pratt's, but to which women may be taken, while every effort is made to cater for private parties which prove a paying proposition. It is all a far cry to the old Carlton of Pall Mall days.

Yet when all is said and done it is as a political club that the Carlton will stand or fall, and such being the case it is no exaggeration to say that its future rests as much with the Conservative Front Bench in the two Houses of Parliament, the Whips, and the Party machine as a whole, as with the committee for the time being. We have seen how close was the connection of the Party with the Club over a long period of years, and those were the days of its greatness. Granted all the difficulties of running any club in the closing decades of the twentieth century it is impossible to resist the conclusion that if the old and close connection with those responsible for the destinies of the Conservative Party is revived, there is no reason why the Carlton should not play an important part in the political life of the country for many years.

Appendices

APPENDIX I

The Original Committee

Trustees

Duke of Buccleugh
Marquess of Londonderry, G.C.B.
Earl of Verulam
Viscount Lowther

Committee

Marquess of Salisbury
Marquess of Chandos
Marquess of Graham
Earl of Clanwilliam
Earl De La Warr
Earl of Falmouth
Earl of Rosslyn
Earl of Wicklow
Lord Granville Somerset
Viscount Maitland
Viscount Stormont
Lord Ellenborough
Lord Saltoun and Abernethy
Lord Stuart de Rothesay
Lord Eliot

Sir Robert Bateson, Bt., M.P.
Hon. William S. Best, M.P.
Sir George Clerk, Bt., M.P.
Sir Thomas Fremantle, Bt., M.P.
Right Hon. Henry Goulburn, M.P.
Sir Alexander Gray Grant, Bt.
Right Hon. Sir Henry Hardinge, Bt.,
    K.C.B.
Hon. Lloyd Kenyon, M.P.
Winthrop M. Praed, M.P.
Philip Pusey, M.P.
Charles Ross, M.P.
W. E. Tomline
Sir Richard R. Vyvyan, Bt., M.P.
Charles Baring Wall, M.P.
Sir John Walsh, Bt., M.P.

Secretary

Mr. James Jephson

APPENDIX II

Chairmen of the Carlton Club

The Right Hon. Lord Claud J. Hamilton, M.P.	1913–1918
The Right Hon. the Earl of Kintore, G.C.M.G.	1918–1923
The Right Hon. the Viscount Younger of Leckie	1923–1929
The Right Hon. the Earl of Clanwilliam, M.C.	1929–1946
The Right Hon. the Lord Sandford, D.L.	1946–1956

215

The Right Hon. the Lord Soulbury	1956–1965
The Right Hon. the Lord Grimston of Westbury	1965–1971
The Right Hon. the Lord Tweedsmuir	1971–

APPENDIX III

Secretaries of the *Carlton Club*

James Jephson	1832–1846
William Rainger	1846–1862
Colonel Sutton	1862–1877
E. Manners Sutton Chichester	1877–1887
A. N. Streatfeild	1887–1912
Walter H. Matthews	1912–1919
Ashley J. S. Morris	1919–1922
Jenkin Lloyd	1922–1926
Brigadier-General Baird	1926–1931
Lieut-Colonel A. L. Y. Willis	1931–1941
Peter Stewart	1941–1956
Colonel Walker, Acting Secretary for 6 months	
Wing-Commander S. P. Angus Bousfield	1957–1961
Major Norman Dicks, M.C.	1961–1963
Michael R. D. Lord	1963–1971

Honorary Secretary

Rolla Rouse	1971–

Index

INDEX